ALL CHANGE AT WORK

ALL CHANGE AT WORK

The Human Dimension

Theon Wilkinson

Institute of Personnel Management

Phototypeset by HBM Typesetting, Lancashire
and printed in Great Britain by
SRP Ltd, Exeter, Devon.

British Library Cataloguing in Publication Data
All change at Work.
  1. Personnel management. Implications of technological
innovation
I. Wilkinson, Theon
658.3

ISBN 0-85292-414-3

CONTENTS

Acknowledgements

This book has been prepared under the auspices of the Institute's National Committee on Employee Relations by a working party composed of the following members:

Bill Mitchell (chairman)	Consultant and until recently Personnel Director, Martin the Newsagent plc
John Brandis	District Personnel Officer, Wycombe Health Authority, High Wycombe
Frances Buckler	P & IR Planning Manager (Scotland), Rolls Royce plc, Glasgow
Norman Dickinson	Employee Relations Manager, Northern Ireland Electricity, Belfast
Richard Holden	Personnel Director, Scottish & Newcastle Beer Production Ltd, Edinburgh
Joan Keogh	Associate Tutor, the Centre for Continuing Vocational Education, University of Sheffield
Ray Milton	Acting Director of Administration, Swansea City Council
Colin Pope	Deputy Director, Engineering Employers' London Association
Matthew Reisz	Commissioning Editor, IPM

– with the chapter on Payment Systems contributed through the National Committee on Pay and Employment Conditions by:

Ken Birkett	Consultant and until recently Chief Manpower Adviser, Anglian Water
and Steve Palmer	Former Manager, Pay and Employment Conditions, now Assistant Director, Development, IPM.

The book was compiled by:

Theon Wilkinson   Manager, Employee Relations, IPM.

The working party is particularly indebted to the research and case study work carried out on the Institute's behalf by Elizabeth Oakley, Research Officer of Incomes Data Services Ltd, which forms the basis of the publication.

This book is the work of many people and has resulted from the support of a number of organizations – in particular, those organizations represented in the 16 case studies at the end of this volume who gave so much of their time over a long period; their help is gratefully acknowledged. In addition, the following eight organizations provided material assistance at the research stage which has been of much value to the working party when assessing the evidence: Austin Rover; Exxon Chemical Olefins; Carrington Vyella; East Cumbria Health Authority; Guinness; Massey Ferguson; STC Components; and Southern Water. All are warmly thanked.

Introduction

A few years ago (1986) the Institute, through its National Committee on Employee Relations, completed a joint survey with Industrial Relations Counselors Inc of the USA on 'The impact of Robotics on Human Resources and Employee Relations'. This was confined to the manufacturing industry and raised so many interesting and far-reaching questions on the changing role of personnel management that it was decided to carry out a further research project on a far wider basis (services and finance, retail and distribution, public sector and utilities, etc.) covering *all* forms of significant change due to the introduction of *all* types of new technology.

The remit of the working party was as follows: 'To research, analyse and report on the impact of changing technology on the field of personnel management with particular reference to employee relations and management/trade union relationships.'

A questionnaire was first devised around six key areas emerging from the robotics survey, to be tested in interviews with senior personnel executives in organizations covering a cross-section of industry and type of technology change. A prototype of the questionnaire used by the research officer in 24 visits is given on page xv and the resultant case studies follow this format, as do the chapter headings.

Each chapter was drafted by one or two members of the working party drawing on as many relevant inferences and comparisons as possible from the case studies; thus John Brandis and Frances Buckler undertook Chapter 1 on Organizational Change, Norman Dickinson and Joan Keogh Chapter 2 on Employee Commitment, Colin Pope and Richard Holden Chapter 3 on Trade Union Reactions, Ray Milton Chapter 4 on Displaced Workers, with a final chapter on the Personnel Mangement Role by Bill Mitchell. Chapter 5 was contributed by IPM's National Committee on Pay and Employment Conditions. The working party retained an overall focus in every section on the effects of any identified change on the personnel management function.

An explanation of the significance of these key chapter/case study areas may be helpful at the start.

1 *Organizational Change* It was found, in the words of Professor Roy Helfgott* when presenting the results of the joint 'robotics' survey, that

> Computer-based technology is having a profound effect upon the ways in which manufacturing operations are structured, the work environment, the nature of jobs, and the ways in which work is organized. It is not the sole factor impacting on each of these, but it is the most important. Furthermore, it is the introduction of new technology that presents the occasion for introducing organizational changes as well.
>
> In brief, the major change in organizational structure is a more integrated one, demanding greater cooperation among units comprising a manufacturing operation. A second change is toward a flatter structure, with fewer layers between the top and the bottom of the organization. A third significant area of change is in the role of supervision, encompassing both its technical and human resource functions. With respect to the latter, what is emerging is a less directive type of supervision and a greater emphasis on communication and advisement.

If this is true of robotics in the manufacturing industry, to what degree is it also true of changes taking place through *other* applications of technology in *other* sectors? The 16 case studies provide an answer.

2 *Employee Commitment* One of the most surprising findings of the robotics study was the extent to which management is being converted to a belief in employee involvement. There was overwhelming agreement (96%) that 'the intelligent introduction of robots to the manufacturing scene makes it imperative that employers take employees into their confidence at every stage'. And, with a new emphasis on the individual, it was considered more important to gain employees' understanding and acceptance than trade union co-operation.

Professor Helfgott had this to say:

> Employee involvement and expansion of the scope of jobs are

* Distinguished Professor of Economics, New Jersey Institute of Technology, and Director of IRC.

becoming increasingly important, because highly automated plants have a growing amount of integration and coordination at lower levels, pushing decision-making downward. Information, formerly a monopoly of managers, may become available to workers on the shopfloor, enabling them to act on their own. The discretionary parts of jobs increase and employees must diagnose problems in order to prevent system interruptions, which are extremely costly under automation. Indeed, some plants are moving toward a new type of job – an operator/maintenance category.

Again, an assessment of the extent and significance of this trend is provided in the 16 case studies and the commentary on them.

3   *Trade Union Reactions* The trade union priorities in the UK were identified by the robotics survey as, first, 'to enhance general job security for members in the longer term' and, second, 'to ensure jobs related to robotics remain within their jurisdiction'. These aims, as might be expected, conflicted at times with management's need for rapid change; yet research revealed an almost total *absence* of union resistance to technical (as opposed to organizational) change:

> In only one case was there a strike, and that was not over the introduction of numerically-controlled machinery centers, but over the manning of those centers, an example of the failure of management to adequately plan and communicate with the union. Indeed, this plant was a very good illustration of internal management conflict. Employee Relations does not understand the thrust of the new technology and Manufacturing lacks understanding of the complex of problems involved in changing people and existing ways of doing things, particularly when they are institutionalized in a collective bargaining agreement with a union set in its ways.

The way forward to less adversarial union/management relationships with respect to changing work practices was found to be through a much greater use of communications:

> Effective communications programs have convinced employees and unions that computer-based technology is neces-

sary to make the firm competitive, and thus enable it to provide jobs for the bulk of its present work force. The communications program must give advance notice of impending change, including information of its nature, the date of its inauguration, the effects it will have on the employees, and the ways in which the company plans to aid those who might be adversely affected by it.

Confirmation or qualification of these trends is looked for in the case studies presented here. In addition, there was a check on union attitudes to employee involvement, which were found in the robotics survey to vary from 'active advocacy to forbidding their members to participate'.

4   *Displaced Workers* Some job displacement was inevitable as a result of the introduction of robotics, but the survey indicated that its effects could generally be managed because of the long lead times required to bring sophisticated forms of automation on line. It was agreed that some displaced workers would need to relocate, transfer to new fields or accept lower-paying jobs, but with a positive retraining policy most displaced workers could be redeployed within the given organization. Training and retraining is the key. As one person put it, 'If you think education is expensive, try ignorance!' Training, moreover, must be conducted at all levels, from top managers to production workers, since the work of all of them is affected. There is, however, one sobering finding: 'Forty per cent of respondents agreed that in the more distant future (2025) it is conceivable that more advanced technology could replace almost all operatives in manufacturing.' The case studies provide additional evidence about areas outside the confines of manufacturing where there have been significant *increases* in employment as a consequence of changing technology.

5   *Payment Systems* The changes induced by robotics affect not only the design and organization of jobs but also the payment system. As Professor Helfgott outlined in his report on the survey:

The nature of jobs and their designation and organization are changing in response to computer-based technologies. The traditional system of work organization, in which jobs are arranged in a hierarchy of distinct, often multiple, classifications, each of which is assigned a separate wage rate, no longer fits the needs. Since the entire emphasis is on flexibility in manufacturing, there has to be greater flexibility in the utilization of the work force. Rigid demarcations give way to more multi-skilled types of jobs, and compensation systems are revised to reward workers for broadening their knowledge bases. Hourly employees gain greater control over their work and are given more authority.

Motivational and reward systems also are in flux. As machine productivity becomes divorced from the actions of individual operators, traditional incentive systems, based on the individual's output, go by the board. Everyone is groping with how to reward people's efforts, which remain important to the efficiency of system operation, but are no longer measurable.

This important chapter examines the search for new compensation and payment systems with particular reference to the case studies.

6   *Personnel Management Role* The impact of changing technology is considered separately in relation to the above key areas; the final question is common to each: 'What were the implications for the personnel management function?' The last chapter attempts to pull this together as a central theme, building on the findings of the robotics survey. This had indicated a number of trends which amounted to a re-writing of the personnel professional's agenda. The enormous scale of investment required imposed a new emphasis on long-term strategic planning, with the personnel management/human resource element involved from the start. This in turn called for a new urgency in training to ensure efficiency and flexibility, and the need for a co-ordinator where employee communications and involvement were concerned. New approaches were also required to recruitment, out-placement of surplus employees, buying in specialist skills on a contract basis, less adversarial trade union negotiations and working in an 'organic' management team. In the words of the robotics report:

Introducing computer-based technology thus poses new chal-lenges to the human resources function. Intensive efforts are required to prevent disruptions within the existing work force while retraining employees for the demands of the new technology. Technological change also presents new opportunities for the employee relations function – to change the way work is organized, to achieve involvement of employees in pursuit of enterprise goals, and to reverse the traditional adversarial labor-management relationship. Companies that have made the smoothest transitions to, and reaped the most benefits from, new technology have been the ones that have included human resource planning as an integral part of their overall strategic planning for the introduction of new products and processes.

The 16 case studies (cross-referenced in *italic* in the text) and commentary reveal the extent to which these trends apply to other sectors – retail and distribution, services and finance, public sector and utilities – and the emergence of new trends.

The Research Questionnaire

General
a) Background of Organization
    Industry or service group
    Size (total employment and financial turnover)
    Location of operating units
    Workforce composition and trade union representation
    Structure of the Personnel Department

b) Introduction of Technology
    Description of introduction within last 3 years
    Comments on any problems in the introduction
    Changes in organization implemented – short term
    Changes in organization proposed – longer term

1. *Organizational Change*
    a) What kind of organizational change took place as a direct result of technological change (job redesign, additional shift-work, etc)?
    b) What is the response of different sections of the workforce to changes in their work and to changes in the organization?
    c) What was the effect of such change on the personnel management function?

2. *Employee Commitment*
    a) Has there been evidence of improved communications and greater use of employee participation schemes?
    b) What evidence is there of a development of employee attitudes towards a more 'working together' approach?
    c) What were the implications for the personnel management function?

3. *Trade Union Reactions*
    a)   Was a New Technology Agreement negotiated or amended?
    b)   How co-operative has the union(s) been to changes in work and changes in the organization?
    c)   What is their attitude to short- and longer-term issues?
    d)   What were the implications for the personnel management function?

4. *Displaced Workers*
    a)   To what extent were displaced employees redeployed within the organization?
    b)   What type of re-training was offered?
    c)   Were significant changes made to a previously established redundancy scheme?
    d)   What were the effects on the work of the personnel management function?

5. *Payment Systems*
    a)   Has there been any re-structuring of payment systems as a direct result of the introduction of technology?
    b)   What has been the effect on grading structures and job evaluation schemes?
    c)   Has there been any change to performance related pay?
    d)   Have there been any moves towards harmonization?
    e)   What were the effects on the work of the personnel function?

6. *Personnel Management and Overall Changes*
    a)   At what stage was the Personnel Department first involved in the introduction of technology?
    b)   Have there been any changes to personnel management policy?
    c)   What changes in personnel management practice have been introduced in industrial relations procedures?
    d)   Has there been a change in techniques of recruitment and selection?
    e)   Has the profile of the workforce changed in the proportions of skilled to unskilled, part-timers, full-timers, job-sharers, temporary and contract staff?

Overall assessment of the impact of technological change on personnel management and employee relations.

1 - ORGANIZATIONAL CHANGE

'Everything flows and nothing remains unchanged.' So spake the ancient Greek philosopher, and he added 'You cannot step into the same river twice.' Our own studies show companies in a state of change like rivers which flow in a constant state of flux and are never the same again. These rivers are now in flood.

It is well to keep this analogy in mind when we consider the questions which form the basis for this chapter.

Does new technology lead to change or does change call for new technology? Can we identify the start or end of a change? Is there dramatic change or continuous change, and how do employees react to both situations?

What can we learn? Can employees be prepared for change? How should manpower resource management react, or should it be proactive?

What kind of changes should we expect from the introduction of new technology? What options are available?

What order can we detect in the change process? What planning should take place? What evidence do we see of planning the technology, planning its introduction or, more fundamentally, planning to prepare people to accept any new technology?

When we examine these questions in this chapter and throughout the book, we will be noting that answers emerge from the case studies in differing ways. Each case study has its own character and excitement and any abstract must be viewed in the light of the background from which it emerges. After all, they do span a broad range of sectors and industries, each with their own traditions, and each with their own interpretation of the personnel role.

In each case study, however, we can see what we may call the river effect. In each there is illustrated a sequence of events, but we are aware of the continuous ever-changing flow of events, swollen by streams of influences muddying the waters. Technological change is only one aspect of overall organizational change, and it is difficult to isolate it and its origins and effects. All organizations studied are shown to be in a state of organizational change and all have technological change. In this respect they are similar, and we shall look for common patterns which are susceptible to prediction and planning. We shall see that some planning centred on the technological change and some was more comprehensive.

Inevitably there is an effect on employees, and the human dimension was in some cases taken into account at the outset, in other cases later. Sometimes there was a continuous change process in operation, and sometimes the human values were continuously being taken into account in the form of a set of basic values or a charter. For our first abstract, let us look at organizations which have set great store on providing a set of such values.

During the 1970s, market pressures and concern about delivery and interdepartmental liaison caused *Holset Engineering* to set aside a week to define the company's common purposes. Four basic values emerged. Customer requirements come first; quality is achieved by doing it right first time; problem-solving requires an action orientation; and people make a difference.

The achievement of these values required good communication at all levels and teamwork, helping and learning from each other. Training modules were implemented to spread the gospel to all employees. Flexibility requirements moved semi-skilled employees to skilled areas and vice-versa. Jobs were enriched and older skills were superseded by automation, which required new skills. Those who had experienced mill closures understood business realities, and initial fears that flexibility could lead to unacceptable degrees of uncertainty were dispelled.

IBM's founder established a set of basic beliefs which still permeate the company's culture. These were needed to cope with an environment in which change is the constant for both the company and employees. The organization has to be adjusted frequently to adapt to the fast-moving needs of the information-technology marketplace. This is highly segmented and varies from country to country.

The underlying values are: respect for the individual; service to the customer; and the pursuit of excellence in all tasks. 'If the organization is to meet the challenge of a changing world, it must be prepared to change everything about itself except its basic beliefs . . . There are two things an organization must increase far out of proportion to its growth rate if that organization is to overcome the problems of change. The first of these is communication, upward and downward. The second is education and retraining.'

Change is managed on a day-to-day basis. Members of the planning teams are drawn from the line and from staff groups, including personnel. Business targets are incorporated into business plans and personnel plans. Career flexibility between skills and types of job is an integral part of IBM's commitment to full employment and the company's strategy for dealing with change. Each hiring decision is a long-term consideration. There is also commitment to single status, to a meritocracy, to open communication channels, and to engendering trust and responsibility. The employee-relations system centres on the employee-manager relationship, and its philosophy and practice are imparted in detail to employees at various stages throughout their career.

This is an organization which has structured its organizational systems, including its human resource system, for the express purpose of channelling continuously evolving change. By contrast, at the other end of the spectrum, there are companies which have well-established systems which effectively provide structural inhibitors.

For example, *Reed Corrugated Cases* diagnosed that it had inherited an industrial relations dominated structure which provides resistance to the development of some employee-relations techniques. Plant Steering Committees meet monthly within the framework of an overall Joint Co-ordinating Committee. Although there is an ability to arrive at clear-cut agreements and to provide a highly participative and problem-solving approach, it can be a detailed, time-consuming and unwieldy exercise. Local major and fundamental changes have become inhibited.

Old structures for communication and consultation which suited a static environment need to give way to new structures. The studies illustrate such structures in communications and emphasize local problem-solving in order to cope with the ongoing operation of new techniques. For example, creative problem-solving at *Holset Engineering* has meant that machine operators can be directly involved with the resolving of technical matters alongside engineers.

This company is an interesting example of a traditional engineering company which has successfully integrated an entirely new concept of human resource management into what was previously a 'them and us' environment. The new concepts (which we have noted above) include clear statements of common purposes and values. These are manifested in practical terms in the form of team working, communication modules and cross-functional workflow groups.

One interpretation is that the skills change associated with high-level technical change in manufacturing provides the stimulus and opportunity to build on 'working together' concepts. *IBM* (which needed to face up to this earlier) has got a lead, but others are closing the gap.

Technological change has been associated, as one might expect, with major structural change. This provides opportunities for the establishment of the fresh human relations strategies usually associated with greenfield sites. Within *Pirelli General*, the levels of integration facilitated by communication systems have allowed changed concepts of work organization to be developed and implemented. At Aberdare in particular integration means that all work is broken down into specifically designed skill modules which are in accordance with the concept of full flexibility. As employees progress in skill proficiency they are able to acquire additional skills modules. At Eastleigh, the achievement of skill flexibility across the traditionally separate activities of production, maintenance and administrative work is regarded as highly innovative and a quantum leap forward in organizational terms.

Technology has facilitated the expansion of some businesses which would otherwise have found great difficulties in coping with market forces and opportunities. This is particularly so in the finance sector. Until 1976, the *TSB* Group did not make loans and had no business customers. They specialised in providing a personal service to individual savings customers. Now they provide a full range of banking services. A terminal placed on the counter provides access to detailed information about each account. In the future there may be many 'robot' branches. In the back offices automation has had an impact on a number of activities. Organizational change of the most far-reaching nature has come about as the result of market forces, and technology has become the means by which successful adaptation to the market can be effected within the resources available .

Staff have become highly skilled at dealing with customers. They have become confident and efficient computer-aided information providers, and sellers of services. Staff need to be recruited at a slightly higher level and must possess the right temperament. New employee specifications emerge from new responsibilities and include additional personal, character and confidence elements.

As we get further into the detail of the studies, there may be less explicit reference to sets of values, but the requirement for (and development of) comprehensive human resource management becomes self-evident.

Before returning to the mainstream, there are a number of side streams meriting comment in the areas of job redesign, job creation and job and employee flexibility. These flow together with implications for decision-making at all levels.

Job redesign has been fairly widespread, but the pattern varies from sector to sector. It ranges from the assimilation of keyboard skills into existing jobs, including management, to complete job redesign in a multi-skilling environment as at *Pirelli General*.

There is some evidence of job creation. Included is the role of the data-processing expert, evolving as a form of organizational consultant under the name of, for example, Computer Services Manager, Operations Manager, Systems Planner or Information Technology Manager depending on the sector.

There has been widespread and major job change in secretarial and clerical functions. These changes were mentioned by almost every interviewee. Some clerical tasks have been absorbed into the activities of computers in almost every case.

Whilst most secretarial and clerical areas have been upgraded, there has been some dispersal of secretarial-type activities such as word processing into non-secretarial areas. Research staff at *Boots* have developed speed and independence by using office technology in their research environment.

Almost every interviewee mentioned improved access to information due to computerization and the extent of distribution of terminals. Computerization has enabled the redesign of management information systems, as in Southern Water. Here all information is on the updated mainframe and all managers are able to access all databases, with restricted access only allocated to personnel records. Monitoring and measuring at pumping stations are now completed electronically.

In general a number of interviewees thought there were widespread implications for the quality of management decision-making. This includes the personnel function, where the quality of decision-making and planning related primarily to the development of databases in personnel departments. However, this was also associated with the general, upgrading of computerised management information systems, which was seen to have implications for manpower and succession planning as well as for absence control, monitoring of labour turnover and stability, control of wages drift, and training.

For example, in the *S and N (Thistle Hotels)*, the training function has taken full advantage of the sophistication of computer systems, which have had a major effect on the work patterns for front-office booking and billing procedures. Information on training needs formerly inputted into word processors has now been transferred into a computer database. The capturing of career profiles and ambitions has been extended to include waiters and chefs. Staff are placed on lists to denote their preferences, availability and transferability.

Not only has computerization had implications for management decision-making, there have been changes in the levels and degree of employee decision-making. This is especially noticeable in the finance sector. Counter and front-office jobs have significant new elements of decision-making, as described earlier for *TSB*. A counter clerk can key in changes and access all relevant information, whether the customer has a cheque or deposit account. Two computer centres cover the whole country's branches and details of personal loans are handled by the same computer.

Broader based employee specifications are not confined to *TSB*. In *Pirelli General* at Aberdare, for example, these are required for the new flexible patterns of working. The most important new quality required was thought to be an ability and preparedness to learn new things. Flexibility can be regarded as a skill in itself, and one of its most important aspects is the ability and preparedness to work in a team and have a co-operative mentality. Aptitude is assessed by a series of tests on computers, and part of the attitude testing involves the use of psychometric questionnaires. This development is helping overcome at the recruitment stage the difficulty of assessing the ability to work effectively in a team.

The manufacturing sector has seen considerable extension of shift working and the development of more complex shift patterns in order to make maximum use of capital equipment. This has occurred, for example, at *Boots'* s new chemical plant, where the advantages of the new computer-controlled plant have been maximized by continuous working covered by new shift arrangements.

Technology has therefore facilitated the consideration of wider concepts of work and aided the development of flexible patterns at work, not only by shift work but by other means such as job sharing, home working and flexible working hours. *Hampshire County Council* has investigated these areas through working parties. These are questioning the organization's need for fixed rotas, and are basing their considerations on research findings that motivation tends to be higher among staff who have flexible hours and are allowed to take work off the premises.

Multi-skilling in the manufacturing and chemical sectors has led to particular dilemmas associated with the dissolving of previous craft demarcations. This has meant a painful coming to terms with business and economic reality. The movement towards such flexibility has been slowed down in *Pirelli General* for example, where the general union felt its position was being eroded and difficulties were experienced between the general and craft unions, within the maintenance function and between the different craft unions. It has proved difficult to persuade representatives of different staff groups to attend the same meetings.

In manufacturing generally, the first-line supervisors have been increasingly in an organizational vacuum. Upgrading of the task of lower levels of management, in the face of the demands of new technology and the requirement for a different type of supervision, has meant that supervisors' jobs are sometimes thought to have changed beyond their capability to do them. No entirely satisfactory solutions have been agreed.

It will be seen that there are certain generalizations emerging from the studies in terms of organizational change, but attempts to isolate the different factors and to determine cause and effect bring us back to the analogy of the river. We can see in each study a mainstream and the various sidestreams, but each river has an identity of its own, and the parts can be understood only in the context of the whole. As a sweeping generalization, we might say that technological and organizational change appear to be interdependent and are best seen as evolutionary rather than revolutionary. Successful implementation depends upon the extent of organizational and human resource planning and is assisted by commitment to values, which may be identified in the early stages or emerge during the changes.

Some studies, however, reveal that the planning and values were missing or inadequate. This is the measure of the need for the development of more rigorous human resource planning.

2 - Employee Commitment

Introduction

'Good communications and good consultation support good management practices. A good deal of emphasis was placed on effective management for effective integration of technical change' (*Boots*). This extract typifies the fundamental message which emerges from the case studies. It is quite evident, although not unexpected, that communications in its various forms is an important, perhaps the most important, means of fostering understanding at the workplace. Without understanding, securing the positive commitment of employees can be an elusive goal. 'Many difficulties experienced with new technology. . . are often found to be due to a failure of communication. . . and matters can be eased by explanation' (*Woolwich*).

The case studies clearly reveal an awareness that successful change programmes (which can generate apprehension amongst those directly affected) depend upon management's approach to the introduction of change; many address the question of what is good management practice and describe the steps taken to improve managerial competence in this regard. What is also clear, however, is that there is no single custom-built package which organizations can 'take off the shelf', which will guarantee the commitment of the workforce to management's change initiatives, whether it is change of a technological, operational or organizational type. Every organization is different – in attitude, ethos, style, structure, purpose, location, financial well-being, etc – and approaches which take account of what exists within the organization and establish objectives are more likely to be effective in the end.

A number of organizations (e.g. *Northern Ireland Electricity*) carried out attitude surveys aimed at gaining a clearer understanding of their workforces' perspectives and their perceptions of the organization as an employer. Others involved managers in defining the purpose of the organization. At *Holset Engineering*, 'from agreement on a clear state-ment of a common purpose emerged four basic values . . . the customers' requirements come first, quality is achieved by "doing it right first time", an action orientation is required to solve problems and "people make the difference".' As a result, Holset concluded that 'in addition to decisions affecting the organization at the level of technical change . . . the key to the achievement of the basic values was agreed to be good communica-tions at all levels and teamwork and helping and learning from each other'.

Communication and Consultation

The case studies properly reflect the distinction between negotiation and consultation – that is, the difference between matters upon which agree-ment must be reached as opposed to matters on which agreement is sought. What is not so clear in a number of cases is whether organizations use the words 'communication' and 'consultation' as meaning the same thing or whether they intend to draw a distinction between them. In Massey Fer-guson, however, 'consultation is defined as a process of putting forward the case for a proposal, seeking reaction and taking part in a two-way debate and creative problem-solving process on points raised before im-plementation.' A few organizations recognized the need to strengthen this aspect of information exchange, as at *Sainsbury's*, where employees are now being encouraged to 'let their views be known'.

The techniques used in the consultation/communication process varied considerably, as would be expected in such different types of organization. Briefing groups are used by *Pirelli General*, team-briefing by *S & N (Thistle Hotels)*, augmented by monthly consultative meetings at which proposed changes are discussed well in advance of implementa-tion. A new approach to communications linked to team-briefing was being developed at *Holset Engineering*. Quality circles were favoured by *IBM*, problem solving by *Reed Corrugated Cases* and *BOC Transhield*, while *Vauxhall Motors* have introduced a new post, Manager Employee Communications, 'in order to place greater emphasis on internal commu-nications'.

Boots, in explaining their approach to consultation, say that 'the principle of direct participation in the sense of management making every attempt to involve people in deciding how their jobs should be done was employed. Once this principle had been observed most employees were found to be very co-operative with the decisions that had been taken about their jobs'. A number of case studies indicate that other organizations also took the view that it was inappropriate to negotiate on change. Consultation procedures were introduced (or existing ones used) to seek the views of employees on the 'how' implications of technological change; and an open management style which improved the quality of communication was adopted so as to keep staff abreast of what was going on.

The precise content and depth of the consultation processes described in the case studies, however, requires careful examination, as several different philosophies emerge. As previously stated, most organizations were very clear as to what was negotiable and what was not, but the depth and scope of consultation across the organizations studied varied considerably. If we take, first of all, those organizations with New Technology Agreements, we find that matters requiring consultation are closely defined. This is not surprising since such agreements were the outcome of negotiation with the trade unions. *TSB* and *Swansea City Council* are examples of organizations which have New Technology Agreements; while the elements of consultation are not completely explicit, it appears that these agreements require management to consult on issues such as:

- a definition of the technological change proposed, together with the extent of its impact on existing processes and working methods
- the foreseen effect on manning and job grading levels
- how excess manning problems will be tackled
- training or retraining proposals
- health, safety and ergonomic issues.

Clearly the implications of some of these matters impinge upon the negotiating processes and would presumably be dealt with separately in the appropriate forum.

A number or organizations have adopted the view that technical change should be treated no differently from other types of change and so have not entered into New Technology Agreements. Examples are *S & N (Thistle Hotels)* and *Boots* who say that '. . . if a [New Technology] Agreement had been negotiated . . . it could be interpreted as an acknowledgement that technical change issues were disproportionate in degree to the real issues experienced in the organization'. *Boots* also express the view, taken by other organizations, that existing arrangements give sufficient commitment to consultation in any sphere of change.

What we see, therefore, is consultation taking place on technical change both under New Technology Agreements and without such Agreements. Other forms of change are dealt with in a similar way to technical change, whether or not New Technology Agreements exist.

Turning to the question of timing, we again see a variety of practices. A number of organizations adopt a more open style of management and go to their employees at a very early stage on all types of organizational change, including technical change. These include *TSB*, where special consultative arrangements were set up to embrace the 'concept, planning and implementation' stages of change. A different approach is taken by *Boots* where 'consultation tends to include more about the "how" (of technical change) and less about the "what" and "when" '. Similarly, Southern Water consult 'before technical change is introduced . . . on the nature, extent, purpose and timing of any changes'. In other words, such organizations *communicate* what they wish to change and *consult* on the effect and timing. The evidence is that this approach has also worked well, probably because it is accompanied by an effective system of communication and because potentially contentious issues such as manning levels, pay and health and safety matters are covered by policies and agreements which remove many of the anxieties felt by vulnerable employees.

It is interesting that the case studies reveal no evidence of disruption being caused by ill-timed change proposals. There are a number of reasons why this might be so, but one can readily call to mind instances where workplace problems *have* been caused by otherwise reasonable proposals being badly timed and where an information vacuum has been allowed to develop, which then makes it more difficult to achieve understanding.

Consultative Arrangements

All of the case studies mention the existence, in one form or another, of consultative arrangements. They include formal well-established structures with a number of tiers *(Woolwich)*, informal arrangements, which are nonetheless regarded as important and involve regular meetings *(Security Express)*, consultative meetings with full-time trade union officials, and those with no union involvement at all *(IBM)*. There is also evidence that some existing consultative arrangements were revitalized by the commitment to consult fully on technical change, and that structures were

strengthened to ensure that consultation arrangements on proposed changes
were fully met, as at *TSB* and *Reed Corrugated Cases*.

There is little evidence to suggest, however, that the larger employers surveyed tend to be those with highly formalized consultative structures and that the small employers adopt a more direct approach to
employee consultation. There is also little to suggest that organizations
where trade unions have a high profile possess more effective consultation
arrangements. In addition, there is no way of measuring the effectiveness
of the variations in approach. What *does* emerge from the case studies is
that each organization has introduced and developed procedures consistent with its own separate needs. All demonstrate a genuine desire to
communicate and consult and in many cases to adopt a more participative
style of management – whether with union officials, staff representatives
or employees – and have put in place arrangements which meet their own
requirements. It is worth noting that most, if not all, of the organizations
would agree that the employees who 'need to know', and whose contribution to the success of proposed changes is therefore sought, are those who
are directly affected by the proposed changes. Where consultation procedures require discussions with representatives of the workforce, as distinct
from the employees directly affected by the proposed change, steps were
taken by management to keep the workforce informed of what was
happening, for example by newsletters and briefing sessions.

As well as demonstrating a belief in the value of fuller and more
effective communication and consultation, a number of organizations
have made further strides towards fuller participation; the adoption of the
problem-solving approach and quality circles (as used by *IBM* and *Holset
Engineering*), which involve employees in seeking solutions to workplace
problems by tapping into the fund of experience available within the
workforce, are examples of greater participation. The sense of purpose and
enrichment which this engenders amongst the workforce is seen by
organizations who adopt this approach as an indication that their management style is bearing fruit.

Attitudes of Employees

It is inevitable that limitations will exist in studies of this nature, and
caution needs to be exercised especially when commenting upon the
employee perspective since the data collected for the case studies de-
pended heavily on a management input. Nonetheless, a number of quite

consistent themes emerge from the studies.

There seems to be a general acceptance throughout the case studies of the inevitability of technological advance and the consequent need to accept and adapt to change. There is also evidence that a greater understanding of the competitive environment in which the organization operates and its financial state are aids to management in securing greater commitment to change and 'pulling together'. These points are best made in the *Holset Engineering* case study and also emerge from the capital-intensive organizations which operate in a highly competitive market, e.g. *Vauxhall Motors*.

A number of case studies provide clear evidence of positive attitudes amongst employees. In *Security Express* we observe that 'some new technology was accepted by employees on the grounds that it enhanced their jobs, and . . . added something to improve their security'. In *Boots*, 'most employees were found to be very co-operative'. In *Hampshire County Council*, the introduction of technology was supported because 'they [employees] understood it to be part of the organizational change which was linked to changes in service provision' – that is, technological change was seen as benefiting the service provided to the community. And in a number of organizations employees welcomed the acquisition of new skills required by technological advance as making them more marketable to other prospective employers; measures therefore had to be taken to retain them. To develop this theme, many of the organizations surveyed negotiated flexibility agreements as part and parcel of technical change. While some reference is made to inter-union rivalry, many employees (especially the younger ones) embraced the widening of their job content and the associated training willingly. The allegation that changing technology 'dehumanized' work is obviously unfounded in these examples, since greater job variety is often the product of increased job flexibility, with the attendant benefits of job enrichment and greater satisfaction.

It is difficult to comment on different employee attitudes within the same workforce. Many of the organizations surveyed employ a significant number of both female and part-time employees. One organization, *Security Express*, commented that 'women were found to be more amenable than men to changes in their working practices as a whole, and to adapt more quickly'. (It is interesting also to note that 40% of this organization's employees are female; the majority perform clerical duties and approximately half are employed on a part-time or seasonal basis.) Why male/female attitudes should be different in this example is a matter for conjecture, and no general hypothesis can be formulated from the information provided by the case studies. The question must be left as an interesting discussion point.

Line and Personnel Management

Perhaps the most important feature to emerge from the case studies in this context is the redefinition of the role of line management. Many of the case studies identify a need to develop a more open management style (from first-line supervision upwards). Line managers are specified as having responsibility for communicating directly with employees. *BOC Transhield* refer to 'the principle of an open style communication' and say that 'managers' Job Specifications require that they be flexible, adaptable and good communicators'. Similarly, in *Pirelli General* it is stated that the 'responsibility has been given to management to develop the skill of face-to-face communications'.

While training is regarded as of vital importance in developing the necessary skills (and also as part of the communications process), the point is also made that recruitment requirements have to be revised so as to ensure that people possessing abilities and personal characteristics compatible with the organization's style of management are selected. In *Pirelli General* the point is put very aptly: 'most [foremen] . . . have had a considerable level of difficulty in adapting to the demands of new technology. Their difficulties in adaptation have been twofold. Some have had difficulty with the "technical" aspects of technology, but almost all do not have the qualities required that would enable them to satisfactorily fill new management posts.'

As well as redefining the recruitment criteria for managers, reference is also made to a more scientific approach to selection, in that attitude testing has been introduced along with psycho-metric questionnaires. Personnel management, therefore, has a key role to play not only in providing training and development programmes designed to improve the skills and effectiveness of managers and supervision at all levels, but also in looking again at the basic job requirements, recruiting people with the desired attributes and potential, and providing suitable management succession plans.

There is evidence too that, arising from the more open and participative management styles outlined in the case studies, the way in which the personnel function is carried out has been undergoing subtle changes. The need for central specialists in personnel management remains, although perhaps fewer than before, but the tendency for personnel people to work as members of multi-discipline teams and for the personnel role to become part of line management is apparent. At *Boots*, the view was expressed that 'the role of personnel is rather more proactive than reactive . . . Greater attempts are being made to incorporate personnel into the business planning . . . line management should have their own personnel manager so that "plans before problems" and "answers before problems" can be jointly agreed'. They believe that such locally based 'generalists' would encourage managers to communicate with their staff and carry out an 'active employee relations policy'. This approach is taken even further in the *Pirelli General* case study, where it is stated that 'the personnel role was to emphasize the business environment in which *Pirelli* had to continue to operate and to hold informal meetings wherever possible with trade union representatives'.

The evidence, therefore, is that such organizations are placing greater emphasis on the 'employee relations' approach as distinct from the 'industrial relations' approach to winning greater employee commitment. A consequence of this is that direct communication with the workforce is augmenting communication with elected representatives, upon whom too much reliance in communicating management's message to the workforce has been placed in the past *(Northern Ireland Electricity, Pirelli General)*.

The *Vauxhall Motors* case study aptly describes what has been taking place: 'The Personnel function . . . is becoming more action orientated. A major objective will be the better utilization of employees with appropriate motivational, training and development programmes. Technical change has assisted the recognition by the company that it cannot introduce equipment alone in order to make progress. A planned approach to the introduction of change, taking into account the human implications, is vital. Thus the involvement of Personnel at the "sharp end" is necessarily enlarging considerably.'

3 - Trade Union Reactions

In recent years, the microchip has made possible technological advances that would have been unthinkable a decade or two ago. New opportunities in all sectors of industry, commerce and the public service have been opened up. The pace of change is exciting, but to some it can also be disturbing and threatening.

New technology has made possible advanced techniques of manufacturing. It allows managers to be provided with fuller and better information on which to base decisions. It has meant that public authorities can offer improved services to the community. However, there has also been a fear, particularly on the part of trade unions, that substantial investment in new technology will inevitably mean that large numbers of unskilled and clerical jobs will disappear forever. This dilemma gave rise to the *New Technology Agreements* (NTAs) of the late 1970's and early 1980's. Ironically, in traditionally unionized areas, such as the factory shop floor, technology was introduced on an evolutionary basis as part of the normal routine. It was not here that the calls for NTAs originated, but in the office, where the introduction of computers and word processors threatened to displace many clerical jobs. Unions such as APEX and MATSA negotiated NTAs to regulate the pace of change. A number of NTAs were concluded, but as staff began to appreciate the opportunities that the new technology afforded, and as managements sought to exploit the full potential of technological advances, agreements which tended to freeze the situation were seen to be inadequate to the pace at which technological change was taking place.

Amongst the organizations featuring in the case studies, one half had some form of agreement covering technical change. *BOC Transhield* and *Hampshire County Council* described their agreements as 'enabling'. Predictably, organizations with the highest union density and involvement were those which tended to have NTAs. However, certain organizations such as *Security Express* operated a closed shop but had no NTA. In some

16

organizations where communication and consultation procedures were long-established, claims for separate NTAs were resisted on the grounds that established procedures for communication, consultation and handling grievances could also be employed to handle any technical change issues.

This approach proved successful in some highly unionized organizations despite the initial wish on the part of the unions to negotiate changes. Furthermore, one company *(Boots)* argued that a NTA would in effect be a distraction from the real task of continuous communication and consultation which was essential to the smooth implementation of rapid technical change. It would also have the effect of singling out new technology from the many other business and economic factors which force change upon an organization and its employees.

The case studies also illustrated the fact that new technology has been introduced with widely differing objectives in mind. Within local authorities it has been brought in to improve the services offered to the community. Amongst companies in the private sector such as *Holset Engineering*, new technology was seen as the means of remaining competitive – and so enhancing the ability of the company to maintain or improve pay and conditions for all employees. As new techniques of manufacturing are introduced, such as numerically controlled machines and flexible manufacturing systems, traditional skills are displaced and total staff requirements fall. The pace and scale of technological change prompted the unions to press for a NTA which gave the commitment to early consultation and the imparting of information throughout each phase of introduction. A job protection agreement was also negotiated in the late 1970's, setting out in detail the measures that will be taken before enforced job losses occur. These included the suspension of overtime, elimination of outside contractors, manufacturing of alternative products, early retirement on a voluntary basis, job sharing and voluntary redundancy. Few of the case studies, however, yielded evidence of agreements which linked the introduction of new technology directly with substantive issues such as pay, re-grading or improvements in other conditions of employment for those employees directly associated with technological change.

From the union point of view, safeguarding health and safety, the provision of training and job protection were the most frequently mentioned aims of NTAs. Procedures for consultation and communication, therefore, characterized most of the agreements described in the case studies.

Technological change has been the driving force behind the more recent TUC interest in promoting Training Agreements. This interest stems from ideas put forward by MSF, whose recent 'Campaigning for Training' initiative set out the arguments for bringing training itself within the scope of collective bargaining. Rapid technological change means that skills quickly become outdated. Union members in mid-career need the opportunity to learn new skills or, in many instances, to begin second or third careers. The union sees part of its role as ensuring that its members' skills remain relevant and suited to the new environment. MSF argues that this is best achieved by entering into Training Agreements with employers through collective bargaining. This approach recognizes that skill shortages are as critical as ever. Furthermore, those in employment today could be those without jobs tomorrow or those who will be forced to take less rewarding employment if their skills become obsolete.

The union makes the point that 'industry and commerce are severely hampered by the lack of adequately trained, professionally qualified and competent staff. Overseas competitors who train and re-train their employees on a regular and planned basis are moving ahead rapidly with new products in important world markets, often at our expense. Many companies are declaring redundancies but have desperate skill shortages. Recruitment of skilled staff in the open market is increasingly difficult and expensive.' Part of the union's initiative is to provide a checklist for members. By scoring the answers to 16 questions individual union members can check how well prepared they are for the sort of work that will be demanded of them in future.

For its part, the AEU has recently launched a series of initiatives designed to put engineers at the forefront of training in industry. The AEU expresses its belief that the success of the UK economy depends on investment in training in the new skills – which is currently quite inadequate to cope with the accelerating pace of change. The union contrasts the number of UK companies stating that skills shortages will impede innovation in products and processes with far fewer who say this in the USA, West Germany, the Benelux countries or Japan. Pilot schemes to provide training in computer numerical control, robotics, electronics and related subjects have been run at three centres throughout the United Kingdom using open learning methods. Union members as old as 60 have responded to the challenges of technological change and have successfully completed the AEU-backed courses.

These initiatives in the field of training all depend on employers or colleges of further education actually providing the means whereby skills and knowledge can be updated. But to what extent should unions themselves be instrumental in fulfilling this role? After all, the original role of the trade unions related to the provision of craft skills. Would it give the trade union movement new purpose in the UK if more unions were to establish and run colleges and training centres under their own control in a manner similar to the EETPU? The EETPU's initiatives in this respect are long established. The union perhaps has an advantage in that it is associated with industries subjected to rapid technological change and recognizes that this requires changing work practices and greater employee flexibility. It sets out to train its members in both technical change and the related areas of organizational and attitudinal change. This approach has won the support of the union's members, employers and Government alike. The EETPU may now be outside the ranks of the TUC but with its investment in training centres and its positive approach to technological change it has succeeded in providing real benefits to its members and industry as a whole.

The EETPU's attitude and philosophy in relation to technological change and the challenge it presents were summarized in an address by the union's General Secretary to a recent NEDO Conference. Countering arguments that trade unions often try to frustrate companies' attempts to introduce change rather than encourage it, Eric Hammond expressed the view that there is little problem in adapting to change when good relationships have been established between companies and the EETPU. His union was more comfortable in pioneering change than just reacting to it.

It also recognized that, for its members to prosper, the industries in which they worked need to prosper. Sadly, this philosophy was by no means universally held within the trade union movement in the UK. The problem is often that constructive moves are frustrated by an underlying historical class-based conviction that the function of trade unions is to fight employers. The EETPU recognizes that commercial success is dependant on the maintenance of competitiveness. This in turn is a function of employees' skills and their adaptability. As a result, there is a need for a joint approach to training and re-training, to multi-skilling, to flexibility and employee involvement. The union had invested significantly in technical training to ensure that its members have the opportunity of enhancing their skills bases.

The union's industrial training service used to offer a course in basic industrial electronics. The service now incorporates one of the union's residential colleges, Cudham Hall, and 12 non-residential training centres located around the country from Motherwell in the North to Plymouth in the South. Over 1,000 companies have bought training from the EETPU and the union has the capacity to provide in excess of 4,000 student weeks of training per year. The programmes are practically orientated and the skills taught relate directly to industrial practice. On any course, the age range can be from the early 20's through to over 50. Based on this training experience, the union is also developing a consultancy service.

For the EETPU, proper training is seen as an integral part of the effective management of industrial and technological change. The union is critical of the fact that too many companies remain unprepared for the training needs they will face. One of the main demands made on companies into the 1990's will be the need for a skilled and adaptable work force. The union argues that the Government should step into the breach where there is inadequate attention to training and insist that companies achieve specified levels of investment in training. Eric Hammond expressed his firm commitment to a consensual approach to the management of change. His union accepted the challenge of the future and the changes that it will bring.

It is significant that the 1988/89 negotiations between the Confederation of Shipbuilding and Engineering Unions and the Engineering Employers' Federation, featured proposals from the unions for a new long-term industry agreement which addressed the challenges of change. On the issue of efficiency in the engineering industry, the unions' proposals included the following statement:

> The prosperity of the engineering industry and the job security of those who work in it depend upon continuous improvements in manufacturing methods, in processes and plant and the use made of them. Technological change and the challenge of international competition demand new skills and flexibility from employers and employees alike.

The same union proposals also addressed the issue of 'Training for Change'. They refer to the skills shortage crisis adversely affecting the productivity of the industry and the job security of employees. They call on employers to join with them in drawing up agreed training programmes whereby the necessary training and re-training would enable all employees to acquire additional and secondary skills. The unions recommended that their members take part in such training and co-operate with management in agreeing to the effective use of training.

This is another example of the recognition by unions of the challenge of change, as a result of technology and competitive pressures, and the need for their members to adapt to the new environment. The New Technology Agreements referred to earlier in this chapter have given way to a broader interest in Training Agreements in response to the pace of change itself, even though their introduction will, no doubt, be subject to tough negotiations.

This chapter has concentrated on the collective trade union response to technical change through negotiated agreements. In conclusion, a summary is given of how organizations featured in the case studies have responded in many different ways to the need to change.

New v Old – Some companies have found a major new challenge in using new technology to increase customer service in a big way *(Woolwich, TSB, Security Express, S & N (Thistle Hotels), BOC Transhield)*. Others may not have had the same motivation *(Boots, Swansea City Council, Hampshire County Council)*.

Industry v Plant – How bargaining arrangements (and pay structures) are determined plays a key role in how effectively organizations tackle change. It appears that the more centralized structures *(Swansea City Council, Hampshire County Council)* have formal NTAs whilst the more plant-based structures *(Vauxhall, BOC Transhield, Pirelli General)* find it more effective to increase the flexibility of working arrangements.

Staff v Hourly Paid – Staff-type organiszations *(TSB, Woolwich, S & N (Thistle Hotels))* appear to take on change more readily than hourly-paid organizations.

Computer (VDU Screens etc) v Machines – There are different requirements from change due to computing technology (employee interface with terminals etc) and change due to investment in process-control equipment. In some ways, this reflects the staff/hourly-paid distinction.

Single Trade Union v Multi-Union – There is no doubt that single-union organizations appear to make faster progress in change implementation. Perhaps, some of the fears of job loss are removed (consider, for example, the newspaper industry).

Line v Personnel – Unless line management 'own' the change process, little can be achieved in practice. The personnel practitioner can negotiate an agreement, the line have to implement it.

Multi-site v Single Site – It is interesting to note that some organizations operate different philosophies in their approach to change at certain sites *(Vauxhall* Joint Venture, *BOC Transhield* at Thatcham, *Pirelli General* at Aberdare). This suggests that many factors are at work in determining the strength of management's will to achieve change.

These factors are important in understanding the environments in which change can be effected. The role of the personnel manager is to create and foster the appropriate environment.

4 – Displaced Workers

This chapter has been divided into a number of sections which arise from an analysis of the case studies in respect of manning levels.

Organizational Change and Technical Change

The issue is complicated by the fact that job loss is often caused by organizational change which may or may not be related to technical change. A further important factor is change brought about by market forces. Technology facilitates re-organization but it is questionable as to how much impact technology has on the decision to re-organize in the first place. *Pirelli General*, for example, quote changing market circumstances and major capital investment as the reasons for a reduction in their workforce and, in common with many other companies, used early retirement schemes to release the bulk of their displaced workers. In a setting where the age structure of the workforce is such that early retirement or voluntary redundancy schemes can be effective, these are clearly the most painless ways of producing a slimmed-down workforce.

In most of the case studies, the companies involved claim to have a policy of non-compulsory redundancy. In the *Vauxhall Motors* case study, for example, it is clearly stated that no employee has been displaced by technology to the extent of being made compulsorily redundant – even though fairly considerable job losses have been experienced. Where the reduction in the labour force could not be achieved by other methods, however, compulsory redundancy had to be used as a last resort.

There are many instances where organizational change has coincided with, or been immediately preceded by, technical change. In these cases it is difficult to determine whether job loss was because of the introduction of a new organizational structure or the introduction of new technology. A prime example of this is the *TSB* case study, where much of the impact of the re-organization was felt by the senior staff.

Technology and Displacement

Holset Engineering summarized the complexity of the relationship between technology and employee severance: 'Whilst technology doesn't necessarily create jobs and may involve some job loss, if technology is *not* introduced, more widespread job loss is likely to result.' This is amplified by the *Woolwich* view that information technology is changing the character of certain jobs so that jobs which are lost in one area are created in another. This enables those staff whose jobs are disappearing to have skills tests in order to identify their suitability for re-training, particularly in the data-processing areas of work. But, once again, there are staff reductions by natural wastage and transfer.

Manufacturing and Services Sector

Running through all the case studies has been underlying concern, particularly of the various trade unions, about the 'net job loss'. Every job which has become unnecessary is seen as a loss to the general stock, but the same emphasis does not appear to have been placed on jobs which have been *created* as a result of new technology.

At *BOC Transhield*, as a result of technical change, 'the equipment planners occupied an organizational vacuum when their jobs effectively disappeared'. The displacement of these workers was handled in a number of ways, which included redeployment and voluntary redundancy. This may be contrasted with *S & N (Thistle Hotels)*, where the introduction of technology has never been regarded as a manning issue, either by the hotel management or the employees. Computerization has been regarded as an opportunity to improve customer service rather than an opportunity to reduce manpower.

It is very noticeable that actual job losses have tended to be fewer and slower in clerical and office areas than in manufacturing. This could be accounted for by the many references to new technology being introduced to cater for an increased workload as an alternative to taking on more people.

Methods of Handling Displacement

It is apparent that, no matter what type of commercial enterprise or industry is being considered, the methods employed in reducing manpower tend to be the same. Natural wastage and voluntary early retirement schemes, together with redeployment into other areas of work, are the three major methods used. In practically all cases there are 'no redundancy' clauses either written into agreements or tacitly agreed between management and unions, although ultimately, if all else fails, compulsory redundancy is the final remedy.

Of all the methods used, voluntary early retirement schemes perhaps require the most careful handling. The needs of the organization have to be carefully analysed before the scheme is implemented, so that the organization retains those people who are necessary to its wellbeing. It is a pointless exercise to allow people to retire early if they are only replaced by other employees who subsequently have to be made redundant.

The redeployment of existing employees in nearly every case goes hand in hand with a retraining exercise. This can be undertaken in a variety of ways.

Company Training

Some companies are fortunate in having their own training centres, often with a formalized and formally recognized system of training which is disseminated throughout the organization. A good example of this is the *Woolwich*, which combines training and manpower planning. Not only are their specialist trainers responsible for undertaking training, but each of their branch managers has some responsibility for the co-ordination and implementation of local training. Branches are closed for half-an-hour weekly so that staff training can be undertaken. Much of this is based on marrying the skills required for the new technology systems with those required for customer service.

Pirelli General, faced with an almost unique situation in trying to develop a training scheme within their optical fibre manufacturing unit, decided on a policy of first recruiting supervisors, who were then required to design their own training system and act as trainers themselves. In order to achieve this, engineers were sent to Japan for two months to gain the necessary knowledge.

External Training

There are many instances where the initial training was supplied by the manufacturer or supplier of the equipment that was purchased. This was usually undertaken by arrangement with either the line managers or the supervisors, and not as part of the normal system of the organization. External training of this type has its own problems, particularly in an office environment where concentrated training takes place at the outset, but many facets of the new systems may not be used until some consider-able time in the future. It is, therefore, very important to define – and cost out – the training required in advance.

In-house Training

The need to provide training geared specifically to the organization, and the cost of obtaining the necessary level of training from external sources, has led many organizations to opt for the in-house or hands-on training system. This can be supplied from a variety of sources, and many organizations have found it expedient to set up their own training facility equipped with the necessary machines and run by their own staff. This sort of facility soon pays for itself, particularly in those areas where continuous training or re-training is necessary. It also has added advantages for companies seeking to redeploy staff in cases of job losses.

General

Many of the companies considered that the importance of training was greatly enhanced in the context of the introduction of new technology. This is particularly relevant to the re-training of displaced workers.

Vauxhall Motors, for example, considered that the 'process of coming to terms with technical change has led to a greater realization of the importance of training as a personnel function'. *Reed Corrugated Cases*, on the other hand, believed that, whilst new technology seemed initially to involve new skills, it also displaced some of the old skills; it was, therefore, necessary to have considerable debate concerning the nature of skills' changes. This led them into the situation where the re-training for process employees was completed on-the-job under the direction of the plant manager whilst a major training initiative for engineers (mainte-nance craftsmen) required off-the-job training.

The emphasis on training as an alternative to redundancy is of great significance, as is the reference to the role of line management in carrying out the training *(Pirelli General* and *IBM)* and the enhanced role of personnel management in manpower and succession planning. Two contrasting approaches to technology displacements can be found in the *Boots* and *IBM* case studies.

Each organization has adopted an approach which is appropriate and successful in their own particular circumstances and focuses on the individual employee, yet they are very different in broad philosophy. At *Boots*, there has been a recognition that their traditional employment security policy has been overtaken by the demands of technical change – which calls for a facing-up to some job loss:

> The need to displace some employees has had the effect of focusing attention on the importance of the manpower and succession planning system, and this function is likely to enjoy something of a higher profile in the future. Displacing employees has also raised the importance of counselling for early retirement. In the last four years job losses have been much higher than at any previous time in the company's history. Counselling can help to spread awareness that the concept of a 'job for life' has now been superseded by events.

IBM, on the other hand, boasts a challenging commitment to full employment secured through a policy of career flexibility between skills and job types:

> The maintenance of full employment is a cornerstone in fostering the acceptance of change. Each hiring decision is a long-term consideration. *IBM* considers it makes a long-term investment in employee flexibility beginning with the recruitment process. Successful applicants are judged to be those who can demonstrate the potential for career flexibility and who will adapt to change . . . Full employment also means that internal recruitment takes preference over external recruitment . . . Employees may need to relocate and to retrain . . . However, the practice of full employment (with its implications of inter-job/department flexibility and retraining), together with the emphasis on advance warning and effective planning, means that organizational safety nets always underpin organizational change.

5 – Changing Technology and Pay

Introduction

When the Institute of Manpower Studies[1] carried out its now famous study of flexible firms, it arrived at the view that labour force flexibility was of three kinds:

- numerical flexibility: the ability to change labour supply at short notice to meet fluctuations in demand;

- functional flexibility: the use of existing (or reduced) labour to carry out a wider variety of tasks; and

- financial flexibility: payment systems which underpinned other flexibilities, in particular by tying reward to individual or corporate performance or a combination of both.

New technology has an influence on all of these areas in the sense that, in *numerical* terms, it gives rise to networking opportunities, shifts and part-time working. In *functional* terms, new technology, which is highly expensive and rapidly obsolete, concentrates the mind on reducing downtime and thus gives rise to the increasing use of previously unskilled or semi-skilled labour to carry out a basic level of maintenance or repairs; it has also led to agreements breaking down the old craft demarcations, which are seen as increasingly inappropriate with the new machinery. Finally, there has been a decisive impact on *payment systems*, with moves towards individualized pay, group bonuses, profit sharing, integrated payment structures and several other options which we discuss later.

What became clear to us in carrying out the case studies is that all of these flexibilities are intertwined, a point made recently by Rathkey and Allen in the conclusion to their analysis of several new technology deals:

> All the rest [i.e. the vast majority] of the companies . . . have realized that the three forms of flexibility are complementary

27

and that, for example, full functional flexibility, which is
aimed at all people working together in groups, is meaningless
if payment is still being made via a traditional PBR system.
Thus, a central feature of many of the agreements is a new pay
system, which may incorporate features of current developments in pay such as merit appraisal.[2]

Certainly, the evidence seems to bear out this analysis of the changes in
pay. According to the New Earnings Survey,[3] some 16.3 per cent of full-
time male non-manual workers receive a form of 'payments by result'
(largely merit pay, bonuses, etc) against just over 7 per cent in 1974. It is
not unreasonable to suppose that this reflects moves away from automatic
increments towards some form of performance-related pay. Similarly, the
recent report on performance appraisal from the IPM[4] concluded:

> During the past decade there has been a substantial overall
> increase in performance review for non-management em-
> ployees: an 18 per cent increase at first-line supervisory level,
> 21 per cent at secretarial and clerical level and, most notable
> of all, a 22 per cent increase at the skilled manual level. There
> was scant evidence of performance review for the latter in
> 1977. *One explanation could be the growing interest in
> flexible work practices and the multi-skilled manual grade,
> which* job evaluation tends to equate *with non-manual techni-
> cal grades* [emphasis added].

Even if performance appraisal has not been translated yet into performance-related pay in all, or even the majority, of cases, it is clearly an
important first step in that direction.

The views expressed so far receive ample support from a recent
ACAS survey[5] of 584 companies looking at changes in flexibility. Their
report indicates: there has been a distinct blurring of the divisions between
manual, technical and clerical employees; nearly a quarter of the firms
used part-time, temporary or sub-contract labour; around a third had
introduced shiftwork; there were moves away from the rate for the job
towards pay systems which encouraged the acquisition of skills; merit pay
had been introduced in a quarter of the companies and another fifth were
planning it; a quarter of the sample had already set up profit-sharing
arrangements and just under a fifth intended to do so; there had been wide
progress towards harmonized terms and conditions of employment.

There may be grounds for arguing that the role of pay falls into the *post hoc* category: something which is changed because of new technology and the concomitant need, above all, for functional flexibility. However, other factors are at work. Individualized pay is as much a philosophical issue, deriving from a management view that individuals should be paid at a rate equivalent to their value to the organization (measured by a mix of corporate and personal performance), as it is an underpinning to changing technology. To assume, therefore, that pay changes are a *result* of changes elsewhere is not necessarily correct; pay can also *initiate* change. In any event, it certainly seems an important means of *reinforcing* change.

Pay and Technology – The Changes

It would be wise to start by stating that the effects on pay of changing technology (and vice versa) should not be overstated. Many organizations in our sample, especially those in the public sector, made little or no change to pay as a result of introducing new technology; others made changes in some areas; whilst yet others made radical reassessments. What follows, therefore, is an analysis of the most frequently recurring features: it is not intended to imply that all organizations adopted all of the approaches described. It should also be noted that there is often no common thread in employers' actions. Two employers may react in a totally different manner to the same issue: whilst one might feel that new technology makes it sensible to extend job evaluation to the shop floor, another may be questioning the relevance of job evaluation altogether. There are no absolutes, and employers should choose a course of action that suits their objectives, culture and employee relations structure.

The major finding from our analysis of organizations who have changed technologies can be summarized as follows:

1 Employers argue that changing technology is not, *of itself*, justifiable grounds for more pay or regrading

2 New technology can lead to the introduction *or* elimination of bonus schemes depending on circumstances. There may be a move away from traditional PBR schemes in favour of group bonus or measured day work

3 New appraisal systems may be introduced with a view to tying pay to performance either now or in the future

4   Existing job evaluation procedures may be reassessed and possibly eliminated or extended

5   There may be a trend away from the 'rate for the job' towards individualized pay

6   Pay may be used to change attitudes and encourage training and career development

7   Organizations may introduce the concept of a craft supergrade

8   Manual and white-collar pay structures may become integrated

9   Harmonization may become an important issue

10 Total working hours may be extended because of a need to work expensive machinery more fully

Let us consider these issues in more detail.

Changing technology does not always mean more pay. Practically all employers argue strongly that changing technology is not, of itself, sufficient to justify more pay and/or regrading. The nub of their argument is that newer technology usually makes jobs less demanding and that increased flexibility enhances the 'psychic' reward through job enrichment. At *TSB*, for example, it was argued that using technology was only part of a job and not the whole of it, and that the overall effect of changing technology was neither to deskill jobs nor make them more skilful, but to change the mix of skills. As a result, in most areas, established differentials have not been disturbed and changing technology has not been a pay issue.

Changing technology does appear in some cases to have led to increased pay and/or regrading, but closer inspection nearly always shows that the real upward pressure on pay rates comes from the labour market – particularly for computer staff. The usual ways around this problem are in evidence, such as the payment of market supplements or setting up of parallel grading structures for staff in occupations with a tight labour market.

Changing technology and bonus schemes. Whilst white-collar employees may seek a 'slice of the action' via regrading claims, manual workers often look to some form of bonus scheme to boost pay. Their arguments are not complex: new technology increases productivity and reduces unit labour costs, and they therefore deserve a share in the gain.

Employers, in reply, sometimes point to the high cost and risk of intense capital investment, and the fact that improvements in productivity are needed to preserve jobs.

When pressing for a 'slice of the action' manual workers will look usually to some sort of group scheme to provide a shared bonus. Whilst traditional payment by results schemes are inappropriate with changing technology and its emphasis on teamworking, fully individualized pay has not yet caught on at this level.

Austin Rover in 1986, for example, replaced the previous productivity and incentive payment scheme with a new plant efficiency bonus. Technical change has been a factor in this move because the introduction of flexible manufacturing systems had focused attention on the need to recognize indirect labour's contribution to production.

Not all employers, however, are keen to move away from PBR to some form of quasi-salaried payment system, because it does mean that pay is also variable downwards. This point was made by IDS.[6]

> Nearly all of the firms seeking to make advances in flexibility have done away with incentive pay schemes and PBR, either moving to a high day rate system or to full salaried status. The inevitable result, especially in industries with sharp fluctuations in demand, is higher labour costs compared to firms with more wage flexibility (e.g. traditional PBR systems).

Bonus schemes of the profit or gainsharing variety do appear to get around that particular problem.

New appraisal systems may be introduced. As we discussed in the introduction to this chapter, one of the features of recent years has been the spread of performance appraisal to manual workers, although there has not been a widespread tying of pay to appraisal at that level. In white-collar areas, where pay and appraisal are substantially and increasingly linked, new appraisal systems are being introduced with the express intention of forging a closer link between pay and performance. At the *Woolwich*, for example, the new appraisal system gives line management a direct link between effort and reward. Assessment is carried out by the line manager and the staff member to give a rating of between one and six under such headings as 'knowledge', 'prioritizing work', 'customers', etc.

Job evaluation schemes may be reassessed or extended. There is no single employer attitude to job evaluation and changing technology. Some employers, those most likely to be pursuing full harmonization, have looked at extending job evaluation down to the craft and manual grades.

Others have seriously started to question whether job evaluation is appropriate for *any* jobs within their organization, arguing that new technology distorts job evaluation factors and imposes unwelcome rigidities by defining individual jobs in terms that make team working and flexibility difficult to attain.

There may be a trend away from the 'rate for the job'. In their report on the flexible firm, IMS pointed to the powerful hold that the 'rate for the job' has on shopfloor thinking. Pay may be variable at that level – but, by and large, only through traditional PBR schemes or in group and not personal terms. However, there are signs that employers are increasingly moving away from the 'rate for the job'. Such a change is a corollary of the 'white collarization' of manual jobs brought about by a combination of managerial philosophy and new technology. It can be recognized in the increasing use of grades for manual and craft workers which allow for some form of progression (often based mostly on service), a rudimentary form of appraisal or skills acquisition.

At Nissan,[7] for example, all employees undertake to operate complete flexibility and mobility, and the range of new skills acquired is a major element in the merit pay scheme. Two grades cover *all* manual employees and in each there is a clearly defined progression related to an annual performance appraisal.

Exxon Chemical Olefins applies a similar philosophy. Great emphasis is placed on career ladders and employees are provided with opportunities and encouragement to make their jobs into careers. Pay for an individual is made up of a number of elements of which the annual salary survey is but one, since individual progress and performance and team performances are also important influences. Salaries are therefore 'individual' and there is no rate for the job.

It is also interesting that whilst Nissan encourages employees at craft levels to become technicians by having no overlap between the traditional engineering and technical grades (i.e. the highest paid craft engineer is always paid less than the lowest paid technician), the highly individualized nature of pay at Exxon leads to grade overlaps of between 50 and 60 per cent so that more experienced people in lower grades may enjoy an initial advantage over less experienced employees in higher grades.

Pay may be used to change attitudes and encourage self-development. Many building societies now have 'true' performance-related pay largely as a result of the need to improve performance and bring about the necessary change in attitudes in a highly competitive industry previously protected by a cartel. At Mars ,[8] on the other hand, flexible pay has been used to change attitudes to training. The company places great emphasis on upgrading skills and has introduced a pay system to reflect this. To rise within a grade, an employee must show an improvement within the job; to change grades, they must acquire new skills.

Introduction of a craft 'supergrade'. Agreements to reduce demarcations between skills have naturally led employers to question the desirability of retaining the old skill distinctions between electricians, mechanics, plumbers or whatever and to consider whether it makes sense to encourage craft employees (and others!) to attain skills in other areas. 'Supergrades', therefore, now often sit on top of an existing craft grading structure. *Vauxhall Motors*, whilst arguing that achieving the same or similar tasks by different methods did not constitute grounds for regrading, accepted that maintenance workers were required to know and do more. A supergrade was created from the staff technical grades but which retained the distinction between craft and technical grades. *Vauxhall* did, however, retain an intermediate grade for maintenance staff with a high level of mechanical skill. *Reed Corrugated Cases* has a similar approach, albeit at process worker levels. Process workers were formerly on a 1 to 4 grade structure which has now, due to technological change, been topped by a grade 5 'supergrade' for central controllers on the new board-making machines.

The introduction of 'supergrades' and other features which tend to blur the distinctions between blue- and white-collar employees can give rise to industrial relations problems, particularly where the changes move employees out of areas traditionally represented by one set of unions into areas represented by another set or no unions at all. Companies can then extend recognition to craft trade unions in staff areas, or encourage employees to transfer to the relevant trade union or become non-unionized. All such options have their problems and require careful thought *before* the 'supergrades' are introduced.

Integrated payment structures. New-technology plants, perhaps because they are often built in green-field sites, have allowed employers and employees to move easily towards integrated payment structures. In situations where both blue- and white-collar workers are paid according to the same principles and within salary structures based on the same philosophy, it appears rational to operate one structure for all employees. At *Pirelli General*'s Aberdare plant, for example, the integrated pay structure is perceived as an integral part of the single union, flexibility and harmonization package that obtains.

On brown-field sites changes of this sort are less easy to introduce, largely because of the traditionalist attitudes of employers, staff and process workers. One obvious step towards achieving full integration is the move being made by many organizations to simplify the number of job titles, grades and pay rates that have built up over the years.

The role of harmonization.[9] A great deal of pay restructuring can be attributed to harmonization. We can further develop the points mentioned above if we consider the fillip given to harmonization by the process of changing technology.

The word harmonization actually covers three different approaches: the gradual elimination of differences between blue- and white-collar workers like separate canteens, clocking on, holidays etc; single status, which means that all employees are treated equally in all aspects of employment except pay; and staff status, whereby certain grades of employees are transferred to staff terms and conditions of employment. The bulk of organizations are at some point on these harmonization roads.

This is usually the result of the need to change shopfloor attitudes in order to ease the introduction and operation of new equipment. Employers who argue that shopfloor attitudes to demarcation, absenteeism and performance pay are archaic are on thin ice if they maintain unjustifiably different treatments of their blue- and white-collar workers. If it is desirable that manual workers should adopt staff attitudes, they are more likely to do so if they are treated as staff. This is particularly evident at craft levels where new styles of working and the responsibilities that go with them make illogical any variations in treatment *vis-à-vis* white-collar workers.

A lot of pay restructuring derives from harmonization. At *Holset Engineering*, restructuring is not a result of technical change but of moves towards greater harmonization. Rolls Royce has seen a gradual move towards harmonized pay and conditions (and some hourly paid groups are achieving salaried status), while at Austin Rover harmonization is seen as a means of moving away from the current spot-rate pay system for hourly-paid employees.

Total working hours may be extended.[10] Whilst this chapter is primarily concerned with the effect of changing technology on pay, mention must be made of one other important area. New technology has had major effects on shiftworking, both in the traditional blue-collar areas and increasingly for white-collar workers such as computer staff.

Expensive and rapidly obsolescent machinery would involve exorbitant unit capital costs if it were not operated at or near its fullest capacity. There has been a move towards the extended working of such machinery either through introducing shiftworking into areas where it did not previously exist or by increasing the existing cover (e.g. by moving from double days to some system of three shifts of discontinuous or continuous working).

Conclusion

There are a number of conclusions that can be drawn. Most obvious is that pay is a crucial *agent for change*, a means of changing employee attitudes not just to changing technology but to their employing organization and its future success. Changing technology relies on a number of factors, not least of which is the co-operation of employees in its profitable exploitation. Pay systems should aim to help maximize that co-operation.

In addition, pay provides an important *underpinning to change*. It helps reinforce messages about individual and group performance, and about flexibility and skills acquisition. Clearly, as we have seen, the payment system can operate as a spur to the provision and taking up of training opportunities, where it links the acquisition of skills to improved levels of pay. At its crudest, pay is just as much a 'bribe' to change attitudes and working practices, and to encourage self-development, as it is a 'bribe' to accept changing technology in the first place.

These twin roles for pay have been helped by a number of factors. First of all, the steady decline of centralized bargaining has prompted a closer examination of local working arrangements and has allowed employers and employees at that level to pursue more effectively their own ends. From the employer's point of view, this has often concentrated on greater flexibility in working practices coupled with a desire to ensure that limited reward resources go to those who have contributed the most. The pressure on employers is to maximize capital utilization via shiftworking and the virtual elimination of downtime, whilst at the same time minimizing labour costs. A side effect of this trend is a massive rise in labour productivity and substantial improvements in pay and conditions for those employees who remain. Surprisingly perhaps, in gaining these ends employers have been assisted by changing expectations amongst employees. White-collar workers seem increasingly amenable to performance-related pay, whilst even if shopfloor workers are not at that stage yet they want a secure pay level with 'earnings at risk' deriving from group bonus schemes rather than PBR. Equally, they seem keen to achieve staff terms and conditions of employment in areas other than pay and prepared to accept the attitudinal changes that go with it.

Perhaps the most important factor in achieving employee acceptance of changing technology is its apparent side effect of bringing about
job enrichment almost by accident. Computerization has freed many
white-collar jobs from their clerical chores, whilst on the shopfloor
changing technology can increase rather than decrease responsibility. To
the extent that new technology can eliminate drudgery, it can also contribute to improving attitudes to work.

The changes to pay that we have considered in this chapter represent
the methods adopted by a number of organizations to use the payment
system to achieve a series of objectives. Others did *not* feel the need to
make changes, and yet others made but minor amendments.The approach
adopted owes much to corporate culture, ethos and philosophy, and these
will vary from employer to employer. The issue is further clouded by
industrial relations factors and the policies, attitudes and objectives of
employees and their representatives. Whatever action was taken at the
organizations in our survey, therefore, it was determined to suit individual
environments. Readers would be advised to keep that point in mind.

References

1   National Economic Development Office, *Changing Working Pat-
     terns: How Companies Achieve Flexibility to Meet New Needs*.
     London, NEDO, 1986

2   Paul Rathkey and Calvin Allen, *New Technology and Trade Union
     Strategy: A Study with Reference to the UK Engineering Industry.
     Final Report of a Research Project*. Stockton-on-Tees, Jim Conway
     Foundation, 1987

3   Department of Employment, *New Earnings Survey, Part A*. London,
     HMSO 1974, 1984 and 1987

4   Phil Long, *Performance Appraisal Revisited*. London, IPM, 1986

5   Advisory, Conciliation and Arbitration Service, *Labour Flexibility
     in Britain: The 1987 ACAS Survey*. London, ACAS, 1988

6   Incomes Data Services, *Flexibility at Work*. London, IDS Study 360,
     April 1986

7   Rathkey and Allen, page 47

8   Incomes Data Services, page 16

9   See Cory Roberts (ed), *Harmonization: Whys and Wherefores.* London, IPM, 1985

10 See Chris Curson, *Flexible Patterns of Work.* London, IPM, 1986

6 - The Personnel Management Role

Many of the major advances and innovations in the field of new technology occurred at a time when the personnel function was facing a new challenge. The power base of trade unions had been demolished by legislation which limited their effectiveness and by the undermining fact of recession, particularly in the basic manufacturing industries.

The emergence of a new brand of line manager, capable and determined to press forward with innovation – sometimes regardless of employee relations considerations but in any event confident in his or her ability to drive through the process of change – gave personnel managers the challenge of re-identifying their role. In many cases, such line managers questioned the value of much traditional personnel practice.

How, then, did the personnel function contribute to the implementation of new technology in the face of a change in its own role in many organizations? Why consult, the line demanded, when there would appear to be no sanctions to back resistance? Why communicate when the end result could be achieved anyway? Consultation and communication imposed delay upon a new, urgent and aggressively impatient breed of line manager, anxious for results in organizations often pressured by City expectations.

Changing shift- and work-patterns, changed employee specifications, transferable skills are all at the heart of the personnel function, but where did the function fit in companies where technical change occurred? What was (and is) its role in this process of change? At what stage in the process of change did (and does) the personnel function come in? Was it in the traditional fire-fighting role, repairing damage from an over-zealous initial approach? Or did the function achieve its long-awaited goal of complete integration into the planning and implementation of the process of change? Did the function operate as an executive arm or just an advisory member of the team? Does the experience of the introduction of new technology point the way to a new role for the function, or is the present situation a temporary staging post with no long-term influence upon the position and status of the function within the management hierarchy?

There were companies where *communication and consultation* were inbuilt into the corporate ethic *(IBM, BOC Transhield)* and as the role of the personnel function was clearly defined and recognized, there was no question that its resources would be needed to implement change. At *BOC Transhield* the Human Relations Charter enshrined communication as a way of life and so the personnel function was equipped to meet the additional load imposed by the introduction of change.

Equally, there were examples in our case studies of other companies in other industries where the personnel function had to gear up to meet a new role, e.g. *Holset Engineering*, where technical innovation led to change in recruitment and training patterns and harmonization of pay and conditions. Even the banking industry, not in the past notable for the personnel function being at the forefront of its business, found a new and important role for communication and consultation.

The onset of new technology undoubtedly gave a fillip to *training and development*, which at long last has assumed its proper major role within the personnel function. Training departments are now seen as vital elements in the employment process, creating skills which may not be transferable to other companies and thereby imparting stability into a workforce which will be at least unwilling (and perhaps unable) to transfer to other companies, to face another training period. Indeed it is probable that most companies would now prefer to retain employees rather than face the cost of training new staff – could this be a new challenge for the (temporarily) recumbent IR specialists?

As employees become less mobile as a result of their skills being related entirely to their particular workplace, they will be unable to move jobs for marginal increases in pay and this will create internal pressures upon employers who may find that they are pressed to respond to minor shifts in the cost of living. Thus a new stability in the workforce will generate a more flexible IR scene and greater emphasis on workplace bargaining.

Trade unions are already finding a new role. The EEPTU (from outside the TUC) and AEU, the MSF and the collective body, the Confederation of Shipbuilding and Engineering Unions, have now changed their ground in terms of opposition to changing technology, looking instead for training agreements to protect their members in their changing jobs.

Unions, therefore, may find, as employees become more identified through their essentially in-house skills to a specific workplace rather than possessing a transferable skill, that their role in representation will wither and be replaced by a new identity as facilitators, creating training and re-training agreements, pension and severance arrangements. It may be that they will even take on training work and develop their own pension schemes to supplement facilities extracted from employers.

Another significant feature of the introduction of new technology has been the effect upon *recruitment specifications*. The *Woolwich Building Society* needed an upward revision of its specification at an early stage to meet the greater demands of the new equipment. This improved specification was limited to some extent by a high stability rate, which increased the problems of the personnel department, faced with both a demand for higher grades of employee and also a low level of mobility and turnover. This naturally led to increased training activity and reduction in the retirement age. New appraisal systems, however, could assist the movement to meet the changed specifications. The result, therefore, was an early recognition of issues requiring the involvement of personnel and training in a sector of business where long-established management style and workforce stability had traditionally held the function in a less dynamic role.

A similar raising of the personnel profile occurred in the *TSB* during the process of technological change, where the function became integrated for the first time into strategic planning with the new increased focus on training. At *Swansea City Council*, the personnel function was also at the forefront of the process of technical change, being involved in the initial stages in the areas of manpower planning and training and retraining of staff.

Beyond this, the function was concerned with the promotion of a *climate* within which technological change could be introduced. The Council had one of the few formal *enabling agreements* negotiated as a vehicle for change. A similar agreement was negotiated between *Hampshire County Council* and NALGO. *Holset Engineering* had a long-standing enabling agreement which was clearly very valuable as a vehicle to smooth the path towards the introduction of radical changes in established engineering working practices.

However, in the majority of cases it appears that no special agreements or processes were created specifically to introduce technological change and that 'normal' consultative and negotiating machinery proved to be adequate. At *Reed Corrugated Cases*, the provisions for the introduction of 'new' technology were an adjunct to the general procedure agreement. *Pirelli General* introduced sweeping changes, including multi-skilling and de-skilling, without the need for special negotiating machinery. *Northern Ireland Electricity* had well entrenched and sophisticated nego-tiating machinery which proved to be quite capable of taking on the demands of the introduction of technical change. Their basic philosophy was clear: change is ongoing and so the latest changes, though perhaps far-reaching, are just part of an ongoing process.

The personnel function has been less affected by the wave of technical change than might have been expected, when the scope of change became apparent in the 1970's and early 1980's. Some of the reason for this undoubtedly lies in the fact that the onset of recession and the arrival of a government determined to regulate trade union power coincided with the technical developments which have flowed through industry and commerce in the last ten years.

During this period individuals have often severed themselves from the collectivist and politically coloured attitudes of unions, aided no doubt by government policies and legislation. It is interesting to note how frequently the case studies reveal that the *workforce* developed an early interest in and commitment to the introduction of technical change.

At the *Woolwich Building Society*, staff saw the introduction of technology as an aid to the removal of the more mundane tasks from their jobs. Checkout staff at *Sainsbury's* felt that new working practices eased physical strain and gave them greater customer contact. At *Security Express*, the changes were seen to offer job enhancement and improved physical security.

Personnel involvement, therefore, was not as centred on the em-ployee relations/industrial relations area as might have been expected. Here line management appears to have taken on the leading role, with the personnel function acting as co-ordinator and advisor. This seems to be part of a general trend – greater power is everywhere being handed out to decentralized line management – and not a phenomenon specifically associated with new technology.

Overall, the main changes felt by the personnel function have been in the areas of training and development and manpower planning. There is a new realization of the importance of the individual (and, no doubt, of the high cost of training employees in adapting to the use of expensive machinery), and this should lead to a greater recognition of individual requirements and the need to explain company policies. This is reflected in the growth of briefing groups and related approaches.

In summary, it appears that the introduction of new technology, together with the changed political climate, has tended to take the personnel function away from the 'front line' – where it has long aspired to be – and back to its earlier roles as counsellor, adviser and co-ordinator. These roles, together with the new realization of the need for the proper training of employee resources, will probably characterize the work of personnel managers to the end of the century.

Boots

Background (May 1989)

The company is one of the top UK multinational manufacturing and retail companies. The company is managed by two prime business executives. In the context of this review the main emphasis has been placed on the activities controlled by the Pharmaceuticals Division Executive.

The Pharmaceuticals Division Executive manages the research, development, production, quality and marketing worldwide of pharmaceuticals, consumer products and speciality chemicals. In addition the Division manufactures a wide range of products which are sold to the company's Retail Division. The Pharmaceuticals Division operations are located in 30 countries of the world. Sales turnover for the year ending March 1988 for the Division was £519.2m with profits of £101.8m.

Employees

Six trade union groupings are recognized. Amongst production and warehousing employees 90 per cent are unionized. Amongst engineering and laboratory staff union density is 99 per cent and 60 per cent respectively. Printing, transport drivers, and shopfitting employees are all 100 per cent unionized. Negotiating groupings are as follows:

USDAW and TGWU represent production and warehousing, MSF represents laboratory staff, and NGA and SOGAT cover printing staff. AEU, EETPU, TASS and UCATT cover engineering staff, UCATT and FTAT cover shopfitters (business recently sold), and TGWU represents drivers. Individual consultations are held with SATA which represents supervisors in factories and warehouses.

The personnel function

Under the Director of Personnel in the Division, the Personnel function is sectioned into five parts. Employee Relations covers industrial relations, welfare and job evaluation. Second and third functions are Recruitment and Training. A manager with responsibility for Overseas Personnel is based in the UK and one manager has responsibility for manpower and succession planning.

Around 70 people are employed in personnel and related work within the Division. Around half of this number are personnel professionals and the remainder are clerical and secretarial support staff. The senior personnel professionals produce policy which allows the company to recruit, motivate and retain staff within the boundaries of what can be afforded in the company's business strategy. Line management have responsibility for carrying out personnel policy. The personnel function has a fairly high profile within Boots with a Staff Director presence on the Group Board.

Introduction of technology

In the Pharmaceuticals Division a new chemical plant at Cramlington in Northumberland has developed advanced batch production techniques. Such chemical production techniques are at the forefront of the available technology and represent a significant leap over previous batch production techniques. Computer controlled and largely automatic, the new techniques can be used either for continuous or batch production. It is likely that the older chemical plants will close with the further development of the new plant.

The pharmaceutical packing lines have been subject to intermittent technical change over the last 20 years. The current high speed computer controlled production lines are seen as an extension of the previous technology rather than a fundamental change.

In the warehouses the manual and clerical tasks associated with order processing have disappeared. The office environments have similarly seen the disappearance of some clerical tasks with the advent of word processors. Typesetting in the printing works has almost disappeared.

Organizational Change

Some job redesign has been consequent upon technical change. However job changes such as these could not be regarded as widespread. Some degree of deskilling was thought to be the result of the advanced chemical production techniques but was replaced by other skills in computer operations.

The advantages of the new computer controlled plant can be maximized by continuous working covered by new shift arrangements. However, the early recognition of shift premiums for key groups of skilled employees has provided the Employee Relations team with a particularly resistant dilemma regarding manning levels. The size of the premiums was initially agreed at rates which have the current effect of making shift work operatives expensive. A medium term solution was introduced but this meant beginning to take employees off shifts altogether. This could undermine the original objective of making the maximum use of the plant through continuous working It has proved difficult to negotiate other options with such a key group of employees.

Word processors have begun to be used by non secretarial staff. Research staff have developed speed and independence by using office technology in their research environment.

Employee reactions

There was perceived to be a marked difference between employees' responses to changes in their jobs and to changes in the organization. The former changes were met by mainly positive reaction but behind some anxiety about the latter was thought to be the fear that jobs could fall by the wayside.

There has been significant movement towards harmonization of conditions and this has coincided with new technology. Clocking in and out has been abolished for manual workers, but with the advent of flexitime for office workers clocking has been introduced for these groups for the first time.

Employee Commitment

The particular strengths of employee communication and consultation strategies go back to 1943 but this was significantly updated in the mid-seventies when the three-tier staff council structure was established. Representatives of the unionized and non-unionized sections of the workforce meet management representatives. The Group Chairman chairs the highest level consultation forum, the Company Central Council. Staff councils can include all matters on their agendas other than those like pay and shift premiums which are specifically negotiated with trade unions.

As the company considers that there is no particular advantage in negotiated change, consultation tends to include more about 'how' and less about 'what' and 'when'. Practices have developed in which most emphasis is placed upon the activities of communicating. Consequently, slightly less emphasis is placed upon consulting and slightly less again is placed upon consultation before the decisions to make changes have been taken. Least frequent is negotiated change.

Good communications and good consultation support good management practices. A good deal of emphasis was placed on effective management for the effective integration of technical change. The policies of a 'cautious' movement forward, and of the careful avoidance of an undermining of the unions, were continued with the advent of technical change.

The principle of direct participation, in the sense of management making attempts to involve people in deciding how their jobs should be done, was employed. Once this principle had been observed most employees were found to be very co-operative with the decisions that had been taken about their jobs.

Trade Union Reactions

Personnel policy centred on strategies that would make the negotiation of a New Technology Agreement unnecessary. An agreement was understood to be an alternative to extensive on-going consultation. Also, if an agreement has been negotiated it was considered that this would not have made any difference to the quality of consultation. Additionally, it could be interpreted as an acknowledgement that the technical change issues were disproportionate in degree to the real issues experienced in the organization.

The main unions, representing their production and warehousing members, submitted a claim for a New Technology Agreement as part of their pay claim in 1982. The company argued, however, that a form of words had already been agreed which provided sufficient commitment to consultation in the event of organizational change. In addition, if there was seen to be a failure to follow through general consultation principles then the grievance procedures could be invoked. The senior representatives had wanted to negotiate change but in the event they reluctantly settled for these principles.

Displaced Workers

ASTMS requested a training agreement at a time when it became clear that some of its members' skills could become redundant.

However, whilst the personnel team was prepared to admit the need for retraining, a full training agreement was resisted on the grounds that full consultation procedures were already installed and there was a commitment to using them to inform and consult on training arrangements. Training policy is to view the re-training needs on an individual employee basis.

Technical change had brought about the need for some job loss. A policy of natural wastage was pursued in conjunction with the Government Job Release Scheme and a voluntary early retirement scheme. The Job Release Scheme was already in existence but proved to be particularly useful for releasing older employees. The voluntary early retirement scheme was brought in by the company as an efficient way of allowing people to retire early. It, of course, could also be related to technical change. Some employees who were considered to be unsuitable or who didn't wish to retrain and could not adapt to new practises were released under this scheme. Around 100 employees per year receive lump sum severance payments, and the scheme has been found to pay for itself within two years.

The need to displace some employees has had the effect of focusing attention on the importance of the manpower and succession planning system and this function is likely to enjoy something of a higher profile in the future. Displacing employees has also raised the importance of counselling for early retirement. In the last four years, job losses have been much higher than at any previous time in the company's history. Counselling can help to spread the awareness that the concept of a 'job for life' has now been superseded by events.

Payment Systems

Considerable productivity improvements have been achieved and technical improvements have made a significant contribution to this. Manual workers' unions have pressed from time to time for more regular performance related and productivity elements in addition to basic rates and annual bonus. It is proposed to undertake research to establish by what criteria elements of performance related pay could operate.

Laboratory staff have pressed for re-grading. A nine-year-old job evaluation scheme is still operating although this may be under review over the next few years. The eight grade points rating system, based on the allocation of points to agreed factors, has seen a steady upward drift through the grades.

Personnel and Overall Changes

Although the initiative for the introduction of technology still rests with line management, personnel professionals have adopted the view that the role of personnel is rather more proactive than reactive as in the past. Greater attempts are being made to incorporate personnel into the business planning. In the future it is likely that directors in line management should have their own personnel manager so that 'plans before problems' and 'answers before problems' can be jointly agreed. In the past personnel people have not been directly integrated at local level. There is a greater need for personnel generalists to be based on site and in the factories and a need for a smaller centrally based team carrying out specialist activities (e.g. professional recruitment and training and developing divisional policy).

The new role for locally based generalists will be to encourage managers to communicate with their staff, carry out an active employee relations policy and ensure organization is correct. Major negotiations may remain centralized and will remain the responsibility of personnel staff. It is personnel's duty to ensure policies and practices are adequate within the context of the business to allow the recruitment, retention and motivation of staff.

There has been a definite trend towards the use of numerically based tests and psychological testing during recruitment for certain jobs. This reflects some of the skills demands of the new technology. There has also been a definite trend towards a smaller core workforce and a larger proportion of temporary workers.

Holset Engineering

Background (May 1989)

Holset Engineering is a wholly owned subsidiary of the Cummins Engine Company of Columbus, Indiana, and has manufacturing and technical facilities in Britain, the USA, France, Spain and Korea in addition to licence operations in South America and the Far East. Holset is engaged in the original design, manufacturing and marketing of advanced specialist components to the diesel engine industry worldwide. Holset Engineering is a major supplier to Cummins Engines, Volvo, SAAB Scania, Iveco, Ford, Man, Renault and General Motors.

Cummins Engines comprises the Engine Division, Components Division and the new Business Division (finance and consultancy). Holset is a major part of the Components Division with engineering facilities based in Huddersfield and Halifax. These facilities are self contained operations incorporating engineering, production, buying and marketing. The Head Office is at Huddersfield.

Holset is a market leader in the design and manufacture of turbochargers mainly for truck engines. It is also the world's leading manufacturer of torsional vibration dampers (viscous and rubber) for truck, car and marine applications. Flexible industrial couplings and specialized rubber products are also manufactured. Air compressors for brakes are exclusively manufactured in the USA. Annual turnover for the operating year 1988 was £50 million for the UK operations.

Employees
UK employees of Holset Engineering number 1,200 with 1,000 based at Huddersfield and 200 at Halifax. Across the company's different functions around 90 women are employed in areas including shopfloor areas. Three bargaining groups, Halifax and Huddersfield AEU and MSF, are recognized covering employees apart from managers and directors. The

49

AEU represents 'works' employees; technical, clerical and supervisory employees are represented by MSF.

Holset Engineering is a single status company with a harmonized grading structure which has been in operation since 1984, covering all employees except managers. Within the eight grade salary structure all employees have salaried status and work a 35 hour week.

The personnel function

At Huddersfield the Employee Relations Manager has responsibility for the personnel operation as a whole. Key personnel professionals reporting to him are the Senior Personnel Officer, the Recruitment and Welfare Officer, the Training Coordinator, Safety Adviser and the Administration Technical Specialist.

Prior to the development of this more integrated structure, the personnel function was organized into Industrial Relations, Recruitment, Personnel Administration and Welfare with Wages, Salaries and Pensions in a separate section.

The introduction of technology

Technical change is regarded as essential to a programme of maintaining the quality, longevity and price competitiveness of products. In very competitive markets in which there is overcapacity in diesel engines, it is vital to look for ways to reduce costs and to achieve faster and improved production.

Holset Engineering has one of the most up to date, flexible manufacturing systems in the UK. This incorporates such features as statistical process control and robotics, and was exclusively designed and built with the expertise of Holset employees. It is interesting to note that the Company has recently been presented with the Queen's Award to Industry for Technological Achievement, linked with this manufacturing system.

Up to 15 years ago all processes were either automatic or semi-automatic. Currently Holset is one of the largest users in the UK of the Japanese Okuma numerically controlled machines. These were introduced in the early 1980s and currently operate alongside some British numerically controlled machines. In common with Huddersfield, the Halifax site has two key production lines although these are on a smaller scale. Automated assembly is now a feature of technological improvement at this site.

The shape of the turbine wheel component in the Holset turbo-charger is of critical importance and the tool grinding process necessary to produce it was formerly a highly skilled and labour intensive task. The grinding process is now computer controlled. In addition, turbochargers have altered in design and components have become smaller with the number of components also reduced. Major improvements in bearings (two are required rather than one) and wheel design, mean that the production process has increased in speed and efficiency.

The material handling area is being revolutionized in concept and practice. The just-in-time principles are being fully implemented to achieve world class manufacturing standards. Materials are delivered, inspected and will then be located immediately onto the appropriate machine.

The office environment has seen increasing levels of computerization, including an IBM mainframe. Buying and production control are all now computerized operations. This has had many positive implications for work scheduling and delivery times. Departments have been able to work closer together, and improved scheduling has reduced time spent in waiting for materials. These factors have greatly improved the delivery times for finished products.

Organizational Change

Bridging the traditional day shift and night shift is a 'middle' shift which commences as the day shift finishes. This has been operating for the last 10 years. The bridging shift is worked by around 50 people who operate the crucial machines and relieve bottlenecks. The need to gain the best advantage from investment in machinery and the production demands to meet greater volumes, mean that more machines are required to be in operation for maximum periods. Thus, with the innovation of the middle shift, this production process is effectively continuous for a total of 105 hours.

The Holset workforce have been required to adapt to changing working practices in two stages of flexibility implementation, first in 1978 and secondly in 1981. Formerly employees were assigned to a machine and had the expectation that they would continue to work with the same machine throughout their working time. In 1978 the flexibility requirements were focused on the movement of semi-skilled employees into areas requiring skills previously associated with skilled status employees. In 1981 flexibility was negotiated for movement in the reverse direction. Thus, skilled employees could be employed in some semi-skilled areas. These changes were introduced as a result of incorporation into annual pay negotiations in 1978 and 1981.

Overall skill patterns have changed in the direction of more 'modern' skills. Older skills such as tool grinding have been superseded by automation but new skills are required to understand and set the numerically controlled machines.

In the office environment more flexibility has been achieved by, for example, the encouragement of an interchange of duties within jobs which were formerly divided into individual jobs.

Employee reaction

Initially employees felt that flexibility could lead to unacceptable degrees of uncertainty. However there was widespread recognition that investment was necessary for the organization as a whole. Living and or working in what was formerly the heartland of the textile industry, many had witnessed its decline. This was widely attributed to lack of investment and those who had experienced mill closures understood business realities at first hand.

There was no noted difference in attitude between younger and older employees with regard to technical change and flexibility requirements. Some employee benefits of change were a degree of job enrichment and 'floating holidays'.

Employee Commitment

During the 1970s Holset Engineering faced increasingly competitive markets and there were some factors relating to cost and delivery which did not match the continuing high quality standard of the products. At the same time there was a recognition that inter departmental liaison was insufficient for organizational efficiency.

In 1983/4 managers and operating managers met in York to define the company's common purposes over the course of a week. From agreement on a clear statement of a common purpose emerged four basic values. These working principles and priorities stated that the customers' requirements come first, quality is achieved by 'doing it right first time', an 'action' orientation is required to solve problems, and 'people make a difference'.

In addition to decisions affecting the organization at the level of technical change, the introduction of numerically controlled machines and statistical process control, a new approach to communications emerged.

The key to the achievement of the basic values were agreed to be, 'good communication at all levels', and 'teamwork and helping and learning from each other'. The intention to raise employees' awareness of what teams can actually achieve was based on the findings that groups regularly achieve better results than individuals in problem solving exercises.

Sources of information for the new approach were derived from Cummins Engines in the USA and the EITB on communications and team building techniques. In-house courses were consequently built up from these materials and presented to managers before implementation.

Employee Development and Communication modules invited all employees, including managers, to attend a three-day training course. This covered such key areas as problem solving, team building, business expertise, and communication skills, in groups of 20. The modules were split between two days in the the first year and one day in the second.

Cross-functional workflow groups operate as quality circles. Problem solving addresses the key issue of how the company can produce greater volume at reduced costs and by easier methods. Engineers discuss design changes in these groups and other employees have the opportunity to voice their own views on design and other issues. The cost benefit advantages of these groups have been found to be considerable in some areas with costs of component production reduced by half. Formerly such employees were not consulted in this way and any opinions or suggestions offered may not have extended beyond the section supervisor.

Trade Union Reactions

A new technology agreement was negotiated in the early 1980s. This gave a commitment to early consultation and the imparting of information throughout each phase of introduction and operation. Consultation was a most prominent activity around the time that the numerically controlled machines were introduced. Emphasis on consultation was found to be somewhat less once the machines had been introduced.

Manufacturing departments have major responsibility for consultation with the shop floor steward in the section. There is no direct personnel involvement although there may be an advisory role.

Displaced Workers

Overall there has been a recognition that whilst technology doesn't necessarily create jobs and may involve some job loss, if technology is not introduced more widespread job loss is likely to result. It was anticipated that with the introduction of the flexible manufacturing system, fewer employees might be required.

A Job Protection agreement was negotiated in the late 1970s. Seven stages were agreed as measures to be taken before enforced job loss occurred. These included the suspension of overtime, the elimination of the use of outside contractors, the manufacture of alternative products, early retirement on a voluntary basis, job sharing and voluntary redundancy.

Payment Systems

There has been no restructuring of pay directly as a result of technical change. The pay restructuring that has taken place is more readily attributable to harmonization.

Shop floor jobs are divided into two categories, semi-skilled and skilled. In addition these employees were formerly paid as either direct or indirect workers. Under flexibility arrangements all employees are paid at direct rates.

Staff areas are evaluated by a joint management and union committee using paired comparisons. There has been no change to the criteria of pay comparisons as a result of technical changes in the office environment.

There are no individual or group incentive schemes. The Holset performance plan is based on the return on sales across the product range and is paid quarterly, to all grades of employees.

Personnel Management

The increasing technical demands mean that recruitment requirements have been revised upwards. New employees are required to have an academic background and ability to the extent that they will be able to enter a BTEC course and later become 'technician craftsmen' for computer aided engineering. In particular they are required to have the ability to work with numerically controlled machines.

There is a preference for candidates with maths and physics backgrounds. They enter a very structured training programme under the auspices of the EITB and after four years can have the opportunity to undertake a sponsored university course. Recruitment into this scheme takes place when candidates are either 16 or 21. A few administrative trainees are recruited at age 18.

One of the recruitment dilemmas arising is that potential candidates with the appropriate level of qualifications are encouraged to stay on at school or college to pursue other qualifications. In addition, despite the technical advantages which have revolutionized the quality of the working environment, the image of the engineering industry as 'oily' and 'unpleasant' persists to the extent that recruitment has to take place against a background of less applications for each post or apprenticeship than is ideally desirable. In addition, airflow (aerodynamic) skills are in short supply as are mechanical engineering skills. Holset is one amongst many employers whose demand for engineers outstrips the quality of the supply.

A number of approaches have been developed to tackle this shortfall. Personal visits to schools are supplemented with discussions with career advisors, the encouraging of females to apply and by visiting the 5 Northern Universities. The dearth of engineering graduates has sparked off considerations of 'golden hello' arrangements. This concept was later dismissed on the grounds that graduates were understood to be more concerned with their long term career prospects than with short term financial gains, and in the event sufficient quality recruitment was achieved.

The company is very conscious of the need to get the right people into the right jobs. This need focuses on people who can take proper advantage of the new opportunities rather than fill craft posts. (The recession had the effect of bringing good skilled labour into semi skilled jobs and Holset thus has ample supply of employees from a craft skill background.) Other important qualifications for the new environment are 'personality' and the ability to work according to new concepts of team working.

Industrial relations remain the main area of activity for the personnel section, and the expectations of the personnel officers' role in providing advice to managers remains high in this area. The job protection agreement and the new technology agreement posed no particular areas of difficulty for the personnel section. The harmonization of pay and conditions programme was more complex. Historically, a fairly wide difference in status had evolved between shop floor environment and staff sections. Those who had made significant achievements on the shop floor had a normal path of progression which promoted them to a staff position and raised their status. The harmonization programme effectively eroded the status differential between the shop floor and the staff areas and some staff resistance consequently resulted. However, resistance was found to diminish over time and no particular additional measures were taken.

IBM (UK)

Background (1988)

IBM United Kingdom Limited is responsible for the UK operations of the IBM Corporation, a worldwide information technology (IT) supplier with some 400,000 employees and a presence in 132 countries. Its 1987 gross revenues of $54 billion put it in the top twenty of the world's largest companies.

Company background internationally

IBM Corporation is organized into four main groupings – IBM United States; Americas Group; Asia Pacific Group; and Europe, Middle East, Africa (EMEA) which contributed some $20 billion to the Corporation's total revenue. IBM UK, which accounted for some £3.5 billion of revenue, is one of four 'large country' operations within EMEA.

The corporation's marketing and customer support activities are carried out nationally; its development and manufacturing are organized internationally. Its UK plant at Havant, near Portsmouth, is IBM's sole worldwide source for the 9335 disk (computer storage) file; IBM UK's Hursley laboratory, near Winchester, has a major development responsibility, outside the United States, for communications and graphics software.

IBM's international dimension applies across its product range. For example, an airline customer might place an order with IBM Netherlands for equipment which uses logic chips developed in France. The chips are incorporated in a 'medium size' 4300 computer manufactured in Germany. Applications software would be developed in Italy; disk files would be manufactured in the UK; and specialist applications would be tested and developed at IBM UK's International Airline Support Centre near London.

IBM UK

The company was established with less than a hundred employees in 1951, when manufacturing of electromechanical equipment started at the company's factory in Greenock, in Scotland. The company's total revenue was just over half a million pounds. By 1981, revenue had grown to its first billion and by 1987 to almost £3.5 billion. Export performance, to which the two UK manufacturing plants made a major contribution, has recently earned the company two successive Queen's Export Awards – the first in 1986. By the end of 1987, the total workforce had grown to just over 18,000.

The company has sales offices in some 40 locations; a research and development laboratory at Hursley; and two manufacturing plants, one at Havant, Hampshire and one at Greenock, Renfrewshire. IBM UK's headquarters, relocated from London in the early 1970s, are in Portsmouth.

The company markets products and services in five broad business areas: information processors from the Personal System/2, IBM's Personal Computer, to the 3090, its largest mainframe processor; telecommunications systems and services; specialist industry systems (such as banking and retail); printers and typewriters; and applications software and services for specialist end users.

The Greenock plant manufactures IBM's PC for the whole European marketplace; it also builds display systems, keyboards and sub assemblies which are incorporated in other IBM products.

The Hursley Laboratory has development responsibility for a range of products including communications and graphics software and disk (storage) systems. Its 9335 system, developed for manufacturing by the Havant factory, won the Queen's Award for Technological Achievement. Another recent innovative product development – for the UK market – was the 4691 programmable cash ('Pub') terminal.

The Havant plant has four main 'product operations'. These are: finance and banking systems, including terminals and automated teller machines; disk storage products; telecommunications products and systems; and a range of display systems and sub assemblies.

Change

A number of factors combine to produce an environment in which 'change is the constant' for both the company and its employees, as IBM adjusts its organization to adapt to the fast-moving needs of the IT marketplace. The products – and the processes by which they are developed and manufactured – are at the leading edge of technology where innovation is 'the order of the day'. It leads to increasingly shorter product development cycles. Innovation also leads to developments such as faster processing, increased storage and improved functions for the same or a reduced price: what IBM and the industry call increased price-performance. This leads to two other linked factors for change. Price-performance improvements increase the scope for commercial and industrial applications and thus widen the marketplace potential. The IT industry, born on the convergence between telecommunications and computers, is dubbed by its commentators as 'the marketplace of a thousand niches'. It therefore attracts an increasing number of competitors. The competitive pressures, particularly in the mid to late 1980s, have led established suppliers, including IBM, to sharpen their marketing strategies and deploy more of their people – and increase the use of 'third party' agents – in marketing activity.

Change makes its impact felt in other major areas of the company. Development and manufacturing 'missions' (responsibilities for particular products or product lines) are co-ordinated internationally. 'New products' may be assigned to a specified laboratory or manufacturing plant – with a corresponding requirement to manage additional skills and processes different from those already in place. And, throughout the company, there is a continuing accent on efficiency which encourages the introduction of new ways of conducting the business. This applies both inside the company and to its relationships with customers, suppliers and other business associates.

One of the company's major strengths – noted by its employees and by industry commentators – is its readiness to change. The company's founder, T J Watson Snr, established a set of principles – called basic beliefs – which still permeate the company's culture today: respect for the individual, service to the customer and the pursuit of excellence in all tasks. He also affirmed the importance of adapting to change, saying: 'If an organization is to meet the challenges of a changing world, it must be prepared to change everything about itself except its basic beliefs.'

Change, it seems, is very much an accepted part of the company's philosophy as well as its business strategy and operations. The company's factory at Havant – focus of this case study and one of the two IBM UK manufacturing plants – has experienced change in substantial measure. The factory site was established in 1966 with less than a hundred employees. In the 21 years to 1987 its employees, now numbering some 1,750, have dealt with a variety of products and have helped introduce different manufacturing methods which now include computer integrated manufacturing (CIM).

Employees

At the end of 1987 IBM UK had on its payroll just over 18,000 full time employees (of which some 2,400 are in management). Around 6,000 are employed at Greenock, Havant and Hursley in manufacturing and development. Some 8,000 work in sales and service support with around 3,500 employed in administration and related functions.

The personnel function

Two central personnel groups, Personnel Relations and Education (including Management and Personnel Development) deal with the longer-term strategic areas of employee relations, education, personnel planning and personnel policy development across IBM. The Personnel Programmes group (covering areas such as personnel information, payroll, job evaluation and salary policy) is also centralized, providing services to all company sites.

Excluding Manufacturing and Development there are about 130 people in the personnel function with between 80 and 90 based in the central groups. In addition, direct personnel support to the main operating units is provided by Personnel Operations groups. In Manufacturing and Development about 40 staff are allocated to each of its three main sites. Here the emphasis is on the role of operational, day to day personnel guidance and support to meet the needs of line management, including communication and education activities.

The introduction of technology

IBM is in the business of developing and producing high technology products by high technology processes. It seems inappropriate to isolate the concept of 'technical changes'; instead this study has chosen to investigate the company's introduction of – and adaption to – change. The intrinsic structure and organization of the company reflect its ever present thrust to seek out positively the business benefits which stem from continuously evolving change. IBM's evolutionary change may be another organization's major change. Structure and organization are built for flexibility.

Product development cycles are becoming increasingly shorter – in some cases two years or less. At any one time many products, some with overlapping cycles, are in production. Thus, flexibility of a high order is required in production techniques and the handling of human resources.

Robotics lines currently represent one of the most advanced production processes in operation. So, too, is Computer Integrated Manufacturing, where further development is already taking place.

The level of computerized support for office procedures, at and between locations, is extremely high and IBM UK now has nearly as many terminals as there are people on its payroll with the introduction of the National Office Support Service. Productivity gains from the system, orginally set at seven per cent per employee, have exceeded expectations. The system supports procedures such as electronic mail, scheduling meetings, and accessing centralized data bases.

Organizational Change

Change is 'managed' on a day to day basis. This is made possible because a focus on the need for change is an integral part of IBM's long-term planning. The planning process is a well-established discipline within and across functions. It is undertaken on a continuous basis but with two key review points – April and September – each year. The Business Investment Cycle takes a strategic view into the future. The Operating Plan – with a two year horizon – deals with more detailed aspects of implementing the company's objectives for the first two years of the strategic plan. The overall strategy, which is effectively updated every year, includes such component features as the communication and education processes involved in change.

It's interesting, here, to note another of Tom Watson's convictions, borne out of IBM's experience as much as half a century ago. He said: 'There are two things an organization must increase far out of proportion to its growth rate if that organization is to overcome the problems of change. The first of these is communication, upward and downward. The second is education and re-training.'

Members of the planning teams are drawn from the line and from staff groups including personnel. Planning for the future – and change requirements – begins with the establishment of business targets. These are incorporated into business plans and personnel plans. Reflected in these personnel plans are the various employee issues which emerge from the manager/employee relationship and other communication channels.

Career flexibility between skills and job types is an integral part of IBM's commitment to full employment and the company's strategy for dealing with change. The maintenance of full employment is a cornerstone in fostering the acceptance of change. Each hiring decision is a long term consideration. IBM considers it makes a long term investment in employee flexibility beginning with the recruitment process. Successful applicants are judged to be those who can demonstrate the potential for career flexibility and who will adapt to change. Accordingly the job in which people enter the company may bear no resemblance to the job in which they complete their career. Full employment also means that internal recruitment takes preference over external recruitment; every effort is made to meet recruitment needs from within.

Havant plant's experience

In a climate of continually evolving change, small scale 'pilots' can be surprisingly indicative of the types of changes acceptable to employees.

At the Havant plant, in 1986, the company built a new 'cleanroom' – purpose-designed to manufacture the 9335 disk file. Some 300 employees work in the cleanroom manufacturing this product for worldwide distribution. Demand reached very high levels in a short space of time. Employees were working lots of overtime but were still stretched to meet volume requirements. Employees were asked to say informally what they thought of the possibility of working continuous shifts and, if so, their preference between eight or 12 hours. In the event, they indicated that continuous shifts were acceptable. They opted for the 12 hour shift because of the extra time off and the premium rates.

Following a preliminary survey, personnel planners and medical representatives joined forces to test out ideas with line managers. The 12 hour shift begins at 7.00am and finishes at 7.00pm (although with breaks employees actually work 10 hours).

It was agreed to run the pilot for an initial period of three months, with extensive testing before, during and after the three month cycle. Testing showed that the pilot was very successful and the cycle was then renewed. This success was attributed to careful planning by the joint team, to the input of the 'medics', who devised break periods in line with the plateau phases in the diurnal cycles, and to the continued dialogue with employees.

Employee Commitment

At the heart of IBM's employment philosophy is the clearly identified basic belief of 'respect for the individual'. To reinforce this concern for the individual employee, IBM has built up a framework of basic principles and personnel programmes: the commitment to full employment, single status, a meritocracy and open communication channels.

The basic philosphy applies throughout the Corporation but is continuously honed and refined to suit the environment of each country. The open communications channels encourage the upward and lateral flow of suggestions for change and improvements. Edicts 'from the top' are fairly rare and usually have the force of saying 'return to the basics'.

IBM is committed to engendering trust and responsibility. Many issues are, in the final analysis, regarded as being part of an individual debate with individual employees. The manager/employee relationship and ratio – the average is one manager to every nine employees – are seen as crucial to maintaining 'respect for the individual'.

IBM centres its employee relations system on the employee-manager relationship. Consequently the identification of potential managers and their training after appointment is seen as of prime importance. Potential managers may have entered the company via a variety of different job categories. Some, but by no means all, joined as graduate recruits. The average length of IBM experience for a newly-appointed first line manager is about nine years.

Managers receive training for effective leadership, good employee relations, and effective two-way communications. They also have a joint responsibility with the individual for the employee's career through recruitment, induction, training, objective setting and career planning. The appraisal of managers covers two areas: the management of people and the management of the task. IBM looks for a sensitive balance between the two – against the backdrop of a fast moving and changing environment.

The employee relations philosophy and practice are imparted to employees in detail at the earliest induction phases and at later intervals throughout the employee's career. The objective is to inform and build commitment to what the company is achieving at the start of the 'mutual contract' of expectations. Whilst employees can expect security of employment, single status, pay and benefits levels above the average, so the company expects an 'above average' commitment from its workforce.

Two-way communications underpin IBM's approach to employee communications. Departmental meetings – normally monthly – provide an opportunity for dialogue and, often, also lead to quality improvement activity.

Employees are certainly encouraged to 'let us know if the system doesn't work'. One of the effects of the well developed appeals and grievance channels is to throw attention back onto the need for effective communication systems and good management.

The self-perpetuating success of employee involvement is demonstrable at the Havant site. About 80 per cent of employees are involved in self-generated quality improvement programmes which have evolved from the more structured Quality Circles of the early 1980s. These are complemented by the company's suggestion programme which continues to pay awards for specific suggestions beyond the employee's own job area.

Issues relating to technical and other change can be channelled through one or more, or a particular combination of, communications channels, including the employee newspaper, bulletin board notices and video programmes. There is a current awareness that it is important not to undermine the line manager's active role by too much reliance on the screen message.

Opinion surveys are carried out for each major operating unit within a two year cycle. The most recent opinion survey in the manufacturing division was completed in November 1987. Surveys give employees the opportunity to express views with the security of guaranteed anonymity – one key aspect of working for IBM. Historically, the participation rate has been high – more than 90 per cent of employees take part.

A core questionnaire of 60 questions was supplemented by a further 30 in manufacturing. The questions help to solicit employee responses to IBM's performance against the three basic beliefs of customer service, respect for the individual and the pursuit of excellence. Other questions solicit views on a range of 'key' subjects including pay, benefits, working conditions, job opportunities, health/safety, communications and management's performance. Employees are also asked how well they think the company is handling change. The answers to certain groups of questions are used to construct various indices which act as a check on the 'health' of IBM's employee relations. The morale index covers the employee's rating of IBM, job, salary versus duties, immediate manager, and opportunity for better job and overall satisfaction.

Answers are coded in numerical terms and comment 'statements' are analyzed separately. 'Trend' data is compared with previous survey results. Results are sent back to line management who are regarded as having ownership of the data. Departmental discussions formulate action plans for the department on the basis of the results. Action plans are also agreed at operating unit level.

Full Employment – Redeployment

The attraction of IBM's commitment to full employment is the security of employment it offers to employees who continue to perform satisfactorily. It also helps to fulfil the strategy for handling change. Employees may need to relocate and to retrain.

Strategic studies begun in 1985/6 and conducted throughout the company underlined the need – and potential sources – for redeployment. Investigations showed the need to rebalance resources to marketing from other areas of the company. By the end of 1987 some 700 employees throughout the company were relocated into 'field' positions with increased customer contact. Following a similar pattern, people in manufacturing have been moved back to production areas from support areas. Relocation assistance was given to employees whose job location was changed and required a house move.

Also as part of resource rebalancing in 1987, under a special programme, more than 440 employees – out of 600 eligible – were attracted by the terms offered for voluntary early retirement. They were all aged 57 or over.

The 'back to the field' programme was a good example of detailed planning and careful management to improve the company's competitive edge whilst maintaining the commitment to full employment. However, the practice of full employment (with its implications of inter job/department flexibility and retraining), together with the emphasis on advance warning and effective planning, means that organizational safety nets always underpin organizational change.

Payment Systems

Salary surveys establish pay rates in comparison with leading competitors for both labour and business. IBM's objective is to pay favourably in relation to this survey base.

The job evaluation structure covers all IBM jobs. Factors in the job evaluation scheme include education and experience requirements, job complexity and accountablility. The scheme measures the relative weightings of these factors in particular jobs.

Job objectives are established for each job in discussions between the job occupant and his or her manager under the IBM Appraisal and Counselling Programme.

Individual job performance is the main factor deciding the amount of salary that individuals actually receive within the appropriate salary range established under the salary survey. Thus the 'pay for performance' policy is applied by manager assessment of performance against objectives.

Salary increases are spread throughout the year and thus there is no fixed annual review date. There are no regional pay variations except for London allowances.

Personnel Management

The manager employee relationship is pre-eminent in the Personnel Management system in IBM. This means emphasis on open two-way communication channels of all kinds and good people management training for managers.

Such is the human resources system, with its safety nets and forecasting, that it is true to say that the stage at which the personnel function is first involved in the introduction of technical change is well *in advance* of the detailed implementation of the change. IBM believes that this is the only way to run its high technology business.

The Manufacturing and Development personnel groups have grown in strength due to the pressure of demands on their services. Senior management recognized the need to meet the increased demands by expanding headcount. Personnel professionals and line management have very complementary and supportive relationships.

One area which demanded increased attention is the management and development of the employee skill mix.

The Havant factory's personnel department has pioneered a skills data base, operational since June 1986. The current plant skills base was already analyzed through an annual survey to categorize employees into five broad skill categories. However, there was no central data base recording previous skills and experience.

The Havant personnel skills inventory data base (PSID) allows employees to input directly into the data base. Information is inputted in uncoded form and covers basic skills, qualifications, relevant external activities, the field in which the individual expresses a preference for working in the future, and a chronological account of all work experience.

The PSID scheme has proved invaluable for building up relevant information on individuals; as tool for management decision-making *vis-à-vis* IBM cross-functional flexibility policy; and as a tool for 'dynamic' modelling according to 'what if?' questions about organizational requirements.

Conclusion

It appears that a key objective is to minimize any gap between philosophy and practice. However, all objectives have to be achieved by securing a sense of employee commitment and responsibility. They work effectively in a secure environment which engenders motivation from a sense of commitment and responsibility.

Pirelli General

Background (June 1989)

Pirelli General is part of Pirelli UK which also has tyre production and cable installation operations in the United Kingdom. Pirelli UK is part of the International Pirelli Group which has operations throughout the world.

Three of Pirelli General's operating divisions are based in the Southampton area with a further division located at Aberdare in South Wales. The heads of these four operating divisions and the company's corporate functions all report to the managing director.

The Power Cables Division is based at Eastleigh. Very large cables are produced here for customers such as the CEGB and Area Boards, with other major customers being the oil industry, British Rail and the Department of the Environment. The export market in the Middle and Far East is also a particularly important part of this Division's trading operations.

The Special Cables Division at Bishopstoke produces a range of specialist electronic wires and cables for military and civil uses, including products for the computer industry. In addition, the Division manufactures a range of fire resistant cables as well as heavier cables for British Coal and the shipbuilding industry.

Also based at Bishopstoke is the Telecommunication Cables Division, producing a range of copper and optical fibre communication cables for use in telephone and cable television networks.

The General Wiring Division is based at Aberdare and manufactures a relatively basic range of 'low-tech' electrical cables which are used primarily for house-wiring and domestic appliances and are mostly sold to electrical wholesalers and domestic equipment manufacturers. Total sales turnover in 1988 was £152 million with after tax profits of £1.8 million.

Employees
The total number of Pirelli General employees was 2,200 at the end of

1988. The largest operating division is the Power Cables Division with 780 employees at the end of 1988. The company's new factory for the manufacture of general wiring cables at Aberdare was opened in 1987 and now has around 150 employees.

Pirelli General has three main bargaining groups. There is effectively 100 per cent union membership (although no closed shop) amongst its hourly-paid production workers, who are all members of the TGWU. Maintenance employees are similarly fully unionized but belong mainly to the AEU or the EETPU. Three staff unions (MSF, ACTSS and AEU (Supervisory)) represent staff employees up to and including first line supervision.

The personnel function

Each operating division has its own personnel department to which the day to day responsibilities for personnel activities are being increasingly devolved. However, the Corporate Personnel Department has retained responsibility for policy formulation and the conduct of companywide negotiations on pay and conditions of employment. This latter aspect has become rather more important since the Company's withdrawal from the Joint Industrial Council for the Cablemaking Industry in September 1987.

The introduction of technology

Pirelli General is becoming increasingly capital intensive and there has been a fairly major investment programme throughout the company over the last few years. Technical change is being introduced on a continuing basis. This often involves improvements to existing machinery but can involve adopting the most modern production techniques and methods of manufacture.

The most clear cut example of this level of technical change is the General Wiring Division at Aberdare. This new factory has a computer integrated manufacturing system which embodies the concept of total integration of the factory's business and operational activities. This very advanced plant has meant that its organizational structure has had to be largely determined by its technology which, for example, includes a data base to which all employees have access.

The Power Cables Division has also seen the pace of capital investment stepped up over the last few years with the introduction of new products, plant and technologies. For example, the equipment in the Submarine Cable Department has been modified to enable a range of new products to be manufactured which will meet changing customer requirements. The computerized preventative maintenance system successfully implemented in the Metals Department will be extended into other departments during the course of the next few years.

In the Telecommunication Cables Division new techniques have been introduced for the production of optical fibres which are increasingly being used by the Division in the manufacture of optical fibre cables for customers such as British Telecom.

Organizational Change

At Aberdare, the level of integration facilitated by its computerized system has allowed different patterns of work organization to be developed and implemented. The work to be undertaken has been sub-divided into a number of skill modules and all employees are expected progressively to acquire and use additional skills both within and across the traditional production, maintenance and administrative functions. This approach will not only increase employee flexibility but will also give employees a better appreciation of the range of skills and activities in the factory and their interdependence.

In the company's other operating divisions, improvements in flexibility have been achieved but these have been less dramatic than at Aberdare mainly due to their more traditional working practices and organizational structures. However, some degree of flexibility has been achieved between production and maintenance operators and between electrical and mechanical maintenance operators.

Shift patterns have been changed or introduced for the first time in some areas in order to ensure the maximum use of new capital equipment and to respond to increased customer demand. In one high technology section where technicians have to work in a dust free environment, the company's normal 12 hour continuous shift pattern was altered to offset the psychological problems that the company felt could result from the long periods of isolation. As a result, a system of four crews working 12 hour shifts has been replaced by one of five crews working eight hour shifts.

Whilst there is considerable evidence of multi-skilling due to the introduction of increased flexibility, there is a great deal less evidence to show that many jobs have been subject to de-skilling. For example, whilst the traditional bought and sales ledger systems have been replaced by new methods, the staff remaining in the accounts function are now increasingly expected to make use of keyboard and information processing skills.

Whilst some jobs are now less physically demanding, other tasks still require fairly skilled manual operations. For example, employees in the Telecommunication Cables Division at Bishopstoke need good hand and eye co-ordination for the manufacture of optical fibres. In other parts of the company, fairly heavy physical work is still a factor in some jobs.

Employee reactions

Employee reactions to increased flexibility were felt to have been fairly positive with younger employees being generally more responsive to change and, on occasions, even welcoming it.

Those who have been given the opportunity to extend their craft skills into other related skills have often seen particular personal advantages. For example, younger electricians who have been trained in electronics now view themselves as more marketable both within and outside the company.

The personnel role

The personnel department has been very active throughout discussions and negotiations on all organizational changes which had manpower implications, and has probably gained a higher profile in the company as a result. Members of the personnel department have led discussions and negotiations with the trade unions during the planning, design and implementation of the measures which have increased employee flexibility.

At the greenfield Aberdare site, change has been its most sharpened and, although the personnel department was not involved at the technology planning stage, it followed very closely behind by developing the associated human resources policies at a very early stage. Before the Aberdare site was built, the human resources policies for the factory were under consideration: visits to other factories in different sectors of the economy were undertaken in order to assess other organizations' practices and experiences in relation to organizational structure, remuneration, flexibility, training, bargaining structures etc.

Employee Commitment

The company's personnel policies now place rather more emphasis on employee relations than industrial relations without overlooking the importance of this latter aspect. For example, the company felt that in the past it had placed too much emphasis on the role of its trade union representatives when communicating with its employees. The current practice is to use direct communications with employees but not in such a way that trade union representatives are excluded from the communications exercise.

Responsibility has been given to line management to undertake regular face to face communication with their employees and, particularly in the General Wiring Division, training in communication skills has been provided for this purpose. In addition, briefing groups have been introduced on an experimental basis in some departments in the Power Cables Division.

When there is the need for written communication with employees on, for example, the introduction of organizational changes or new working arrangements, the personnel department is actively involved in preparing the text and maintaining the quality of written communications.

In the Special Cables Division a well-established practice was broken when the decision was taken to have the representatives of both staff and hourly-paid employees at the same consultative meeting. This practice has not yet been adopted in other Divisions although it remains a serious possibility for the future.

Trade Union Reactions

An area of difficulty for the personnel department in negotiating change with the unions has been the rivalry between the different unions with members in the Company. In particular, difficulties have been experienced between the TGWU and the craft unions, and between the different craft unions. The unscrambling of traditional craft demarcations has sometimes been difficult and time consuming, and the TGWU has felt that the strength of its position in the company has been gradually eroded, especially as job losses have tended to affect its membership rather more than that of the craft unions.

It has also often proved difficult to persuade the representatives of staff and hourly paid employees to attend the same meeting. In attempts to overcome this problem, the personnel department has endeavoured to emphasize business reality and to adopt a policy of greater openness about the business environment in which the company is operating.

No formal new technology agreement has been negotiated but one or two major agreements introducing important improvements in flexibility have been reached over the last four or five years. Much of the unions' concern has been focused on the definition of 'flexibility', on minimizing job reductions and on seeking the company's assurance that any required job reductions would be achieved on a voluntary basis. ·

The most innovative agreement that the company has introduced has been at Aberdare where, after discussions with a number of different trade unions, a single union agreement was signed with MATSA in 1987. This new agreement included a number of new features, including compulsory binding arbitration as the final stage in the negotiating and disputes procedures.

Displaced Workers

Changing market circumstances and major capital investment over the last few years have been key factors in the reduction of the company's workforce to just over 2,000 at the end of 1988 from 3,750 in 1978. Apart from natural wastage, a significant number of employees have left the company under early retirement and redundancy schemes. Due to the age structure of the workforce, it has been possible to achieve most of the required reductions on a voluntary basis.

Employees leaving under these schemes have been provided with counselling by the personnel department as well as, where appropriate, careers advice and financial guidance by professional external organizations.

Where employees have had to be redeployed to alternative positions, they have been given earning protection and provided with both internal and external training to facilitate their redeployment. In particular, a number of older employees have been provided with training in keyboard skills and computer appreciation.

Payment Systems

The company's payment systems have not been significantly changed as a direct result of technical change except at its Aberdare plant. Here, the introduction of an integrated salary structure is an essential and fundamental part of the comprehensive agreement that was reached with MATSA. Under this salary structure, the salaries of employees are increased on an individual basis as they successfully acquire additional skill modules.

Personnel Management

Although the personnel department was not directly involved in the technical planning of capital investment, the personnel implications of such investment have raised a number of opportunities for the personnel department to develop policies at an early stage. This was particularly the case for the new plant at Aberdare.

At Aberdare, the new flexible patterns of working have required the development of somewhat different and broader-based employee specifications. The company's requirements have been sub-divided into 'aptitude' and 'attitude' with, in the latter case, particular emphasis being placed on flexibility, adaptability, and self-sufficiency. The aptitude of potential new employees for the different working arrangements is assessed by using computer aptitude tests with their attitude assessed by the use of psychometric questionnaires.

Another important requirement for new employees at Aberdare was the ability and willingness to work in a team and not to exercise individuality in a way which would jeopardize teamworking. However, it has often been difficult to assess this quality at the recruitment stage since it only really becomes apparent when the employee has spent some time in the new working environment.

In some parts of the company there have been difficulties in both recruitment and training due to the specialist nature of the skills required. An example of the ways that this problem has been overcome is where the company sent some of the staff who were recruited for their Optical Fibre Manufacturing Unit to Japan, since this was the only location where a similar technology could be found.

In addition, the company has on a couple of recent occasions sent a number of production operators to other factories within the Pirelli Group to enable them to train on machines that were similar to those that were being installed.

Supervisors

An important personnel problem that the company has had to face has been the changing role of the first line supervisor. About 10 years ago, the company made an attempt to improve the quality of its first line supervisors, which it termed section managers rather than foremen, but many of these section managers had previously been foremen and had difficulty in taking on increased responsibilities.

Historically, foremen and section managers were generally

promoted from the ranks of hourly-paid production operators but they were often found to have difficulties in coping with the increasingly complex technology in the factory and the need for broader managerial responsibilities. As a result, further re-structuring has recently been undertaken, with many of the older section managers being unable to be placed in supervisory positions in the more streamlined organizational structure.

This has created a problem since the first line supervisors' relatively narrow training and experience has made it difficult for them to be successfully redeployed into other jobs. Furthermore, the new type of supervisors are increasingly being recruited from amongst the company's graduate recruits, with the result that the traditional path by which hourly-paid employees could transfer into staff positions has largely disappeared.

Reed Corrugated Cases

Background (1988)

Reed Corrugated Cases, a former member of the Reed International Group, now Reedpack following a management buyout, manufactures a range of corrugated and printed boxes. Customers include supermarkets who have requirements for a range of boxes including point of sale display cases.

Employees

Employees number 4,000 with 500 based at the Aylesford plant. The largest union at this site is SOGAT which operates a post entry closed shop. 80 per cent of employees are defined as 'process workers' and are represented by SOGAT. The AEU and the EETPU represent craft workers. ACTSF represents around 50 per cent of staff employees.

The personnel function

The personnel function is characterized by a strong central structure. This structure was set up under an agreement known as the Bexhill agreement. Whilst negotiations are carried out centrally and employee involvement initiatives originate from the same source, somewhat more limited personnel support is provided at plant level. Each major factory employs a personnel officer whose role focuses on welfare and some recruitment work.

The introduction of technology

The process of change is regarded as an organic progression of refining existing techniques, with no day to night change experienced. The production process has historically been of a relatively low technology kind. Paper is steam heated, rolled, spliced and corrugated. Over the last five or six years this process has gradually been automated with paper fed in and taken off automatically.

Over the last 15 to 20 years the printing side of the business has developed from letterpress techniques into the flexographic printing process. Under the flexographic process 715,000 cases can be printed per hour rather than 12,000 – 18,000 per hour under letterpress.

Materials handling has been automated with the introduction of robotics and computer set traversa systems.

Organizational Change

The degree of automation has developed up to an intermediate stage. Less physical effort is required for many jobs but some employees still undertake 'heavy' work. It is conceivable that these jobs will be 'technologized out' in the future, although this is not under current consideration.

There has been a good deal of debate at Reed Corrugated Cases surrounding the nature of skills changes. New technology seems initially to involve new skills whilst also displacing some of the old. Technology was not thought necessarily to mean an upgrading of skills. After the period of initial adaptation required the skills themselves were necessarily no longer 'new'. As the effect of the 'newness' subsided, so the debate about the nature of changes was superseded.

There is agreement on the major skill changes involved in the printing side of the business. The flexoprinting, four colour post printing, automatic dye production, APR photopolymer system is regarded as high technology. Previous high skill requirements have consequently been lessened. Formerly, artists, writers and letterpress operators were employed. Whilst artists are still employed their future role could become more 'high tech'. The company is examining the possibilities of computer aided graphics and design. The future adoption of these techniques could change the skill requirements of the artist.

Debate has also focused on the question of into which job or job area new skills should fall. The task of laser cutting 'the form' is a clear example of this. Before the arrival of lasers it was a staff job to design 'the cut' and a process job to undertake the cutting. The removal of former concepts of job demarcation is seen as an imperative for future development.

A new concern with 'line quality' led the company to want to appoint quality leaders. Although technology has always been the responsibility of the machine operator, in the past there had been a tendency for the supervisors to take over this responsibility. With the arrival of new machines the company wanted to appoint machine operators, currently acting as crew leaders, to take on the additional role of quality leaders. Due to the supervisors' established working practices in this area it has not proved easy to achieve this.

Employee reactions

Employees have shown a general acceptance of technology changes. These types of innovation are seen as a way of protecting the future and the rationale for their introduction is accepted as such. Nonetheless, the future possibility of fundamental change arouses most employee concern over job security.

Employee Commitment

The 1973 Bexhill agreement is the key framework for introducing technical and other changes, in addition to dealing with the 'normal' business of industrial relations.

A Joint Co-ordinating Committee meets monthly for a one and a half or two day meeting. Five or six Fathers of the Chapel are present, together with two trade union officials, the personnel director, the industrial relations manager, one executive director and three general managers. The agenda is regarded as open and wide and could include the state of the present market, productivity, technology changes and the 'notes' from the Plant Steering Committee.

Plant Steering Committees meet monthly for three hourly meetings, at each of Reed Corrugated's 12 plants. Participants are the plant manager, one executive manager, a Father of the Chapel, other Chapel representatives and section supervisors. The agenda covers joint Co-ordinating Committee 'notes', plant output and productivity, and can also include, among other subject areas, the Youth Training Scheme, absenteeism and new machinery.

Plant Steering Committees are regarded as a multiple mirror image of the Joint Co-ordinating Committee structure. Whilst historically the operations of this overall structure have achieved some of the benefits of a highly centralized structure, this factor, together with its maturity, is beginning to be regarded as an inhibitor to dealing with change.

The advantages of the structure are seen as the ability to arrive at clear cut agreements, and to provide a highly participative and problem solving approach. Consequently, there is little surprise management. However, it can be a detailed, time consuming and unwieldy exercise.

Also, although the Bexhill structure has facilitated change to date, it could be considered that major and fundamental changes cannot be achieved against the background of the Bexhill agreement structure. A single bargaining structure, for example in a new plant context, could not easily be accommodated.

Communications Groups continue to exist under the PSC structure and meet on an 'as and when' basis. These groups were formerly well developed before the Bexhill structure reached maturity but are now less well used.

Trade Union Reactions

The Bexhill agreement contained many detailed statements on the introduction and operation of technology. The reactions of unions overall can be described as very supportive at plant level.

Displaced Workers

Reed Corrugated Cases has experienced less job loss than other companies in the same industry. However, there have been spasmodic significant redundancies. Severance arrangements were mainly a plant managers' responsibility, but with some assistance from the personnel function.

Whilst the main machines areas have seen expanding work volumes, the future, with full automation of material handling areas, means that the same security of employment cannot be guaranteed for employees in 'service' areas.

A voluntary redundancy scheme operated for those severed from the company due to technical change. The main dilemma associated with this system was that the people whom the company wished would volunteer had a tendency not to volunteer. The skilled employees were amongst those whom the company preferred not to lose first.

Re-training for process employees was completed as 'on the job' training under the general direction of the plant manager. A major training initiative for engineers (maintenance craftsmen) was undertaken in 1985 and involved some 'off the job' training.

Payment Systems

A jointly agreed job evaluation scheme covers all employees except for engineers. This is an 'averaging' system derived from factors including physical effort, mental effort, working conditions, dexterity and co-ordination, monotony levels and skill levels. The staff structure is graded between A and J. There has been a grading drift upwards through the grades and the bottom grades are almost depleted. The job evaluation system was considered to require review every 10 to 12 years.

Process employees were formerly graded on a one to four structure ranging from 'machine man' (4) through to 'assistant machine man' (3) to 'feeder' (2), and 'take-off man' (1). Due to technology and job changes the structure has now been topped by a grade five 'Supergrade'.

The new board making machine requires a central controller designate in the central control box position. Central controllers occupy grade five. One or two other jobs have also been regraded from four to five. The form makers' job incorporates the use of a rotary die cutter and this job has consequently been moved on to grade five via job evaluation. With the development of printing on die printing machines there has been some shop floor pressure to upgrade jobs affected from four to five. However, the company attempts to limit the number of employees who can move into the supergrade.

Personnel Management

Most strategic work of the personnel function is conducted through the central channel provided by the Bexhill structure. The Joint Co-ordinating Committee is the 'powerhouse' of the company, with issues feeding directly into company policy.

The plant personnel officials' role (with one exception) has evolved as low key but with a major emphasis on welfare matters. Training, development and organizational development are currently lower key activities than would in future be desirable. A key reason for this was thought to be the weighting towards industrial relations (IR) activities afforded by the strongly centralized Bexhill structure. A highly developed IR structure together with an underdeveloped plant level structure means that there is little existing structure suitable for effective provision of training, development and other non IR personnel activities. Currently there are some moves to upgrade the plant level personnel function.

Vauxhall Motors, Luton

Background (1988)

Vauxhall Motors is a UK subsidiary of the giant US corporation General Motors, and is its UK car manufacturing division. Vehicle assembly plants are based at Luton in Bedfordshire, and at Ellesmere Port on Merseyside.

General Motors also has a 'joint venture' operation with the Japanese Isuzu Company Motors which is also based at Luton. General Motors has a 38.6 per cent stake in the Isuzu operation in Japan.

Annual turnover is £1,642 million. Currently around 27 vehicles per hour are produced at the Luton plant and 33 per hour are produced at Ellesmere Port.

Employees

A total of 11,044 employees work for Vauxhall Motors: 8,643 are hourly paid and 2,397 are staff. 4,276 manual and 678 staff employees work at the Ellesmere Port plant where the Astra range of cars and vans is produced.

3,733 manual and 1,430 staff employees work at the Luton plant on production of the Cavalier and in central staff functions such as purchase, planning, marketing and finance.

In addition, 634 manual and 289 staff employees operate the Parts and Accessories unit, which is housed in a warehouse at Toddington, and at administrative offices in Dunstable.

A union membership agreement (closed shop) covers hourly paid employees. The TGWU is the largest represented union, with the remaining hourly paid membership divided between the AEU and the EETPU. Staff unions are TASS and ASTMS (now MSF).

The personnel function

The personnel function previously had a highly centralized organization. More recent and current developments mean that the personnel function is following a pattern of decentralization in conjunction with the trend to local decision-making within strategic business units. The decentralization process has been most marked at Luton with the establishment of dedicated plant personnel activity under the manufacturing director. At Ellesmere Port the plant has had more site level organization for some time.

The manufacturing director at Luton now has responsibility for the personnel functions related to all salaried and hourly paid employees within his sphere of responsibility. Recently manufacturing and engineering activities, which were formerly centrally based, have been transferred to plant level responsibility.

The plant personnel manager has responsibility for personnel services for all salaried and hourly paid employees in the manufacturing operation, including employee relations, apprentice and technical training, medical, safety and plant protection, catering, and human resources training and development activities. Some external consultancy work is commissioned from time to time in the areas of training and organization development.

Vauxhall's head office is also based at Luton, comprising the central marketing, public affairs, finance, legal and taxation activities. These functions have their own personnel support services. The director of personnel has responsibility for all industrial relations and personnel policy co-ordination and for management development. A new post has been created at Luton, Manager Employee Communications. A similar position is being established at Ellesmere Port in order to place increased emphasis on internal communications.

At Luton the Training Services activity has a specialized function dealing with the impact of technology in the plant. A training officer is responsible for each of the four manufacturing units, Body, Paint, Trim and Final. They co-ordinate 'on line' and 'off line' instruction.

The introduction of technology

As a subsidiary of General Motors, Vauxhall is subject to a process of 'technical interchange' between the parent's constituent divisions. Technical change can therefore be said to be one of the results of high level corporate strategy.

Car and vehicle manufacturing businesses continue to operate in a very competitive market and there is some over capacity in the marketplace as a whole. Vauxhall is also subject to international pressures arising from fluctuations in exchange rates, for example. Effective utilization of technology and economies of scale improve competitiveness by reducing costs and improving efficiency – in a business environment in which pressures to produce more vehicles, at better quality, on a faster turnaround and at the lowest costs, are pre-eminent.

Computer controlled processes and monitoring equipment have been introduced into the hourly paid areas. Highly integrated processes control, monitor, fault find and display information on screens. These currently employ approximately 1,200 people and assemble the Bedford Midi Van and the Suzuki Super Lorry and Bedford micro vans for sale in the UK and Continental Europe. A second shift is currently being introduced which will bring the workforce to 1,700 people and will eventually double the plant's output to around 40,000 units per annum.

An investment of £68 million in the Ellesmere Port plant in 1984 redeveloped the plant with robotics, new welding and handling equipment, and computer controlled processes being introduced for the production of the new Astra model. However, in the context of the distribution of new technology, this development (like other technical developments at Vauxhall) was regarded as advanced in concept (representing some 'state of the art' developments) but not necessarily in the level of utilization. In 1987 a new paint plant representing an investment of £90 million was commissioned at Luton. This included the most advanced paint plant technology and facilitated a very high level of quality in paint finish.

Alongside such investments as the paint plant, technology is generally regarded as 'model driven'. Whilst technology is becoming relatively cheaper and easier to install and use it is nonetheless difficult to justify its introduction 'midstream'.

A totaly separate joint venture company, IBC Vehicles Ltd, involving General Motors and Isuzu Motors of Japan, has been operational at Luton since the autumn of 1987. This was established as the only viable alternative to a plant closure following sustained losses within the Bedford Van operation. At an early stage the decision was taken to incorporate the Japanese's efficient production system and related expertise into a joint venture at Luton. Features of its operation include just-in-time production, a single status labour contract with minimum demarcations, and worker flexibility. This latter is maximized by the use of manufacturing teams of 10 to 15 people headed by a team leader.

Organizational Change

The levels of utilization of technology are such that the impact on hourly paid staff has not been great. However, input into computers was previously regarded as a staff job and hourly paid employees have some new exposure to input and monitoring activities.

Most job change has been experienced as a result of the new versatility and multi-skilling objectives. A key example of job change affects the maintenance function. A maintenance employee is required to use skills broadened well beyond those of a mechanical fitter. The requirement for the blending of previous job boundaries between electricians and other maintenance workers is a direct result of the technical demands of new equipment.

Following extensive negotiations with the five trade unions, major changes in working practices, pay and conditions were agreed as the condition for the setting up of the General Motors and Isuzu joint venture company. These required worker flexibility within a concept of team-working, a company council for collective bargaining, the introduction of temporary workers, a rationalized pay grading structure, an extended arbitration system, a two shift system and the principle of single salaried status for all employees.

Employee reactions

Technical change was accepted by the majority of employees who were affected by it because it was experienced as taking some of the drudgery elements away from their jobs. On the whole technical change was regarded as evolutionary rather than revolutionary, and employees were thought to experience changes as beneficial provided that they were notified in advance and appropriate training was available.

Employee Commitment

The joint venture operates a plant Joint Company Council Charter. The five unions and management are thereby committed to round-table discussions. Regular and wide ranging consultation covers such areas as new technology and the state of the business. Trade union representatives retain the same status in representative terms as they have in Vauxhall's Luton plant.

Trade Union Reactions

In November 1984 commitments associated with the introduction of a new wage structure for hourly paid employees included a 'General Requirements' section on 'acceptance of new technology in processes and procedures', 'acceptance of broader jobs, particularly by combining existing job classifications', 'flexibility in performing any jobs within employee's competence in the scale', 'continuity of production throughout the shift', 'employee commitments to do the job right first time', and 'the elimination of restrictive practices in overtime and job demarcations'.

A two year offer, to be backdated to September 1987, includes 'versatility' payments for all employees of variable amounts depending on grade, as part of a pay deal combining a percentage increase on basic rates and a consolidated element from existing bonus earnings. Some of the largest versatility increments under the scheme would be for the top skilled grade, with multi-skilling as a final objective, and for the main production grade.

At Luton union reaction was characterized as generally co-operative because the requirement to increase investment was understood. However, most concern was linked to potential job losses and to the implications of 'versatility'. A dispute arose at Ellesmere Port on new working practices for electricians, where the company required an increase in flexibility. This dispute was later resolved and no parallel dispute arose at Luton.

There was some concern amongst unions that practices in the joint venture plant would 'roll over' into the main car operations. There was also pressure to include more people in the new superskill grade added to the top of the craft structure.

A Code of Practice for Ergonomic and Environmental Factors relating to Computer Terminal Workplaces was developed, and provided as an Appendix to the 1983 Agreement. This provided guidelines on environmental or other factors which are recognized as being necessary for the welfare of employees operating computers. Standard guidelines were thought appropriate to ensure consistency of approach in providing facilities particularly with regard to Visual Display Units. The code of practice provides detailed procedures to ensure appropriate conditions of lighting, heat, noise, layout, furniture, screen viewing, eye testing and work patterns.

The 1983 procedural agreement with TASS confirmed that information on an employee's current job performance will not be entered onto computer records without the employee's prior knowledge. Security of personnel files will be maintained and proposals to increase the content of personnel information on computer files will be discussed before imple- mentation. (The company conforms to the requirements of the Data Protection Act in this matter.)

Displaced Workers

Although fairly considerable job losses have now been experienced at Vauxhall Motors since the early 1980s, it is clear that only some of these were indirectly related to the introduction of technology. However, no employee has been displaced by technology to the extent of being made compulsorily redundant.

In February 1983 an 'Agreement on Computers' was reached with TASS. This related to the introduction and extension or modification of the use of computers. The implementation stages of the agreement gave a commitment to inform TASS representatives of the existence of a feasibil- ity study relating to the use of computers which would alter the working conditions or practices of TASS members, and to provide information through line management on the results of any study. Before introducing any change that would affect TASS members' jobs through the use of computers, commitments are also given to discuss with TASS representa- tives the purpose of the computer, revised or additional job descriptions, instruction or training proposals, and redeployment.

The February 1983 agreement also states that there will be no enforced redundancy as a direct result of the introduction, extension or modification of the use of computers.

In a Security of Employment procedural agreement made with ASTMS in May 1982, the company agreed to give as much forward notice and information as possible to trade union representatives in the event of a labour surplus, and certain actions will be taken to minimize or prevent a labour surplus arising: assessment will be made of the likely effect of normal wastage over the period in question; recruitment into the affected job categories will be suspended; overtime in the affected job categories will be jointly reviewed; contract work will be recalled to the extent terms permit where such actions will reduce the impact of the labour surplus situation.

If in following these steps a surplus labour situation is still likely, the company will review with the union the total situation facing the company, the possibilities of redeployment and the opportunities for re-training employees.

If the labour surplus persists the company will advise ASTMS centrally at plant level, consider offering early retirement to affected employees and a programme of voluntary separation after consultation.

Procedures are also laid down for non-voluntary separation, although this has never been deployed to achieve employees' severance directly caused by the introduction of technology.

Payment Systems

Whilst many more employees in staff and hourly paid areas have access to terminals and screens as part of their jobs, the company takes the view that achieving the same or similar tasks by different methods does not constitute a need for re-grading. A process of de-specialization coincides with a process of taking on broader roles, and in general terms this is not considered to lead to the need for payment alterations.

However, it is recognized that maintenance employees are required to know and do more, and for this change the company were prepared to revise pay upwards. A new 'supergrade' was added to the top of the craft grading structure. This was derived from staff technical grades but with the interface between craft and technical grades retained.

An intermediate grade was also created to provide scope to accommodate maintenance personnel with high level mechanical skills.

In an overall pattern in which less junior clerical staff are now employed, as a result of the introduction of office technology, some clerical staff have been regraded in recognition of their taking on broader and more complex skills.

The joint venture van plant has a grading structure which is similar to the Nissan grade structure. It has a simplified salary structure within a single status context and with eight grades.

Personnel Management

The process of coming to terms with technical change has led to a greater realization of the importance of training as a personnel function. At times in the past when Vauxhall was under competitive, financial and other pressures, training activities were amongst the first to be cut.

The training department has recently achieved a stronger role in servicing the needs of manufacturing. In the future it is envisaged that the progressive upgrading of skills could involve longer periods of off the job training. The training department is also expected to have a role in new induction techniques and in the effective integration of new recruits to the company.

Traditionally, recruitment was directly from a local catchment area. New requirements are now for a brighter person with more adaptability and preparedness to be flexible. This new approach requires a revamping of recruitment procedures. Previously, recruitment at a time when labour was scarce had an anonymous flavour and tended not to be specifically focused on the recruitment of individuals. Progressive change is taking place to improve not only induction but also selection procedures. New techniques will include manual dexterity and numeracy tests and team orientation tests for hourly paid operators. In addition, more graduates are expected to be recruited into technical and commercial areas.

The personnel function is considered to be in a transitional phase between a period in which it tended to be administratively orientated, and current and future phases in which it is becoming more 'action' orientated. A major objective will be the better utilization of employees with appropriate motivational, training and development programmes. Technical change has assisted the recognition by the company that it cannot introduce equipment alone in order to make progress. A planned approach to the introduction of change, taking into account the human implications, is vital. Thus the involvement of personnel at the 'sharp end' is necessarily enlarging considerably.

Hampshire County Council

Background

As one of the three largest non metropolitan counties in England, Hampshire County Council provides a wide range of public services to one and a half million people. Educational services cover primary schools, secondary and advanced postgraduate level work, with educational spending taking over half of the council's total annual budget.

The social services committee is responsible for the welfare and protection of children and those who are aged, handicapped and disabled. The Planning and Transportation Committee is responsible for road planning, maintenance and improvements. The County Council acts as agent for the Department of Transport who reimburse the cost of work on motorways and trunk roads. Planning functions include control of waste disposal and mineral extraction, the preservation of historic buildings, archaeology and landscape design.

The Public Protection Committee is responsible for the Fire Brigade service, Waste Disposal and Trading Standards, licensing, certification and for the Coroner's service. The Police Service is provided by Hampshire Police Authority. The Policy and Resources Committee establishes overall policy and controls resources on behalf of the Council. The Land Sub-committee controls the use, acquisition and maintenance of Council land and buildings. The Personnel Sub-committee develops policies for the county's manpower resources. The Recreation Committee's responsibilities include the public library, museums, country parks and archives services.

Employees (1988 figures)

Hampshire County Council is the largest employer in Hampshire with 62,778 staff. Of these approximately a half are full time and a half are part time employees. Occupational groups include lecturers, teachers, social workers, police and fire services. Professional and technical groups include accountants, solicitors, civil engineers and architects, in addition to laboratory technicians, and computer programmers. Other trades and skills represented include various building trades, vehicle fitters, cooks, cleaners and roadworkers. The largest occupational group are teachers and lecturers with over 14,000 full time members. The Social Services committee provides jobs for over 4,700 manual and non manual staff. The police service is the third largest occupational group with over 3,000 employees. Staff are employed at over 1,000 different establishments around the county, including schools, residential homes and local offices. The net budget for 1988 is £900m.

Representatives from 16 unions are members of the Joint Trade Union Committee. NALGO has the largest representation amongst staff with 5,713 members. NUPE and NUT share joint second place with 3,733 and 3,647 members respectively.

The personnel function (as at January 1988, before restructuring)
The central Personnel Department has about 30 professional personnel staff and the departments account for another 50. Most departments employ their own personnel officers. The County Manpower Services Officer has overall responsibility for policy formulation. Three manpower advisors provide advice and support across the range of county activities. The two executive wings of personnel organization are Employee Services and Management Services. Employee Services provide a direct service to the minority of county departments which do not have their own personnel officers, and to all departments on such daily matters as recruitment, discipline, industrial relations and occupational health and safety. The Management Services section has a team of 10-12 consultants available to provide reviews of service delivery and effective use of resources.

The introduction of technology
In the early 1980s Hampshire County Council was operating a growing mainframe computer system but with a relatively small network of terminals. The mainframe was used for certain heavy duty systems: these included the county payroll, client systems and large data bases for road and planning operations. Broad based personnel information was derived from the payroll information.

Developments in technology design and manufacturing meant that less costly systems became available. This meant that opportunities were created for more widespread use of a wider variety of information technology systems. However, the intoduction of a 'distributed' network required careful planning to ensure the most effective development within an organization which essentially operates as a federation of separate companies. In 1982 an Information Network Group was established. This was composed of 15 senior county employees whose task it was to become fully informed about information technology. Additionally their brief was to develop a commitment to technology as a corporate subject independent of any departmental bias, and thereafter to derive broad policy proposals on the strategic direction which information technology was to take within Hampshire County Council as a whole. The Group undertook to run a number of pilot schemes for a corporate data base and for an electronic mail system.

Despite its success the Information Network Group concluded that the further implementation of information technology should be under the firm leadership of chief officers. In 1985 an Information Technology Board was established with its members including chief officers, under the chairmanship of the Chief Executive. The main purposes are to create policy and to communicate with all staff through, for example, newsletters and computers themselves. A separate Information Technology Forum was also established. The brief of this group was active implementation and the solving of day to day problems of detail in relation to technology, through a senior manager in each department. The group had responsibility for the planning of corporate systems including personnel, finance and buildings.

Pilot projects were also carried out including electronic publishing and digital map based information systems. The new personnel management system became available to departments in March 1989. An early commitment demonstrated by departments suggested that they would be inputting personnel data and thus assisting in the early development of the full corporate data base.

In 1987 each department was asked to complete an information technology plan which referred to information technology supporting the basic service needs of the department. It was also to refer to the use which it could foresee of corporate systems such as Personnel and Finance. Plans were completed by early 1988 and a corporate Authority level plan produced by December 1988. The plans are now in their second year and are improving in quality.

The main longer term objective is to link the county's 1,000 establishments to the mainframe computer network and to extend its links to the community and other organizations. This objective is now within sight. The county is now linked into various national databases, provides direct links to Portsmouth and Southampton City Council's mainframes and also links into IBM's local network. Interest is being shown by voluntary organizations and the University so that the network over the next few years will be extended. The notable exception, because of its size, is the Education Department. Although the technology is now available which would allow schools to be included, the limiting factor is the considerable cost of linking each and every school and college around the county.

Current technology has at its centre an IBM 3090 – 200E which carries the main (HANTSNET) information network. The Information Technology Services Section provides additional products and services. These include personal micro computers, the word processing system, systems design and programming, together with training and consultancy services.

Home-working has also been introduced as a technological application providing advantages to both the Authority and to employees who are able to access the developing database. Also gaining some support from councillors is the planned introduction of terminals into the homes of the leading councillors. They could refer to committee papers from home in advance of council meetings.

Organizational Change

The policy approach of members of the Information Technology Board and of other key council employees is one which could be summarized as pragmatic rather than prescriptive. As a provider of public services the distributed information technology facilities were seen to have two main benefits: (1) the improvement of communications for the benefit of customers/ratepayers and (2) improved access to information for council employees. Technology also assists the implementation of the policy of devolution of decision making to separate departments. There can be some value added benefits, notably arising from the use of word processing systems. Technology also has implications for the improvement of service delivery to the public.

Organizational change is primarily linked to service change and technology is used to ease forward the changes that service changes can involve. Prior to 1978 the Social Services Department was organized in three tiers. Over the 1978/79 period the second tier was removed and the available technolgy was used to achieve this. Computer terminals are currently sited on the reception desks of area offices and can be used to give information to the public quickly and efficiently.

Flexibility

A Working Party developed proposals for introducing flexible work patterns and reported in April 1988. Home-working using computers was linked to a wide range of flexible working patterns such as job sharing and flexible working hours including annual hours contracts. Many departments now have people working either completely at home or significantly home-based using electronic links. Also many senior managers have taken to using computers at home. Home links are now being considered as part of the very real recruitment need for scarce specialist staff within the community, particularly with demographic issues being in the forefront of our minds.

1987 was seen as a development year and 1988 and 1989 as years of consolidation, in which the organizational changes being considered will be implemented. Changes are likely to be implemented such that the overall pattern will be one in which the authority's role is managing the provision of public services rather than one of the management of public services. It is forseeable that there will be some growth in the numbers of employees employed on a consultancy basis, although this raises the supplementary issue of how consultants are to be themselves managed.

The introduction of the word processing systems was found to be a value added exercise. Once the system has been introduced, it can then become available for other applications. In this case, electronic mail was a later development which was implemented at minimal cost because the basic technology infrastructure was already up and running. Individual work patterns are not monitored. Technology has not been employed to monitor the quality or quantity of employee output.

Employee reactions

No direct opposition to information technology was experienced from any section of the large workforce. However, it was anticipated that once terminals were introduced into the Education service (and into schools in particular) some difficulties would be experienced. The technology was expected to be met with pressure for time away from normal job duties in order to come to terms with it. Also, there would be increased demand for training in order to close the skills gap which can be found in schools. School children often have a better understanding of computers than their teachers or parents! Terminals in schools can also pave the way for open learning packages and for a possible change in the school day to the continental schedule. There has been significant support from the Education Department in ensuring that all staff within the Department have access to and are aware of issues relating to information technology. The nettle has now been very much grasped both with respect to the curriculum and to the support service needs of both teachers and managers.

Employee Commitment

Full established consultation procedures have been followed in the context of technical change. For example, at every stage of the planning and introduction of electronic publishing, full information was available for employees.

Two county publications have been devised to inform employees about technology developments. *IT News* informs on major information technology developments and on county policy. *IT Update*, a colour magazine, provides features on the use of computers in individual departments. Research shows that the distribution coverage is around 86 per cent of employees.

Trade Union Reactions

Representatives from 16 unions are members of the biannual Hampshire Joint Trade Union Committee. The introduction of technology has never arisen as an organizational issue isolated from other issues at this meeting. All unions could be described as generally supportive to information technology although NALGO, as the largest union at Hampshire County Council and the union representing a large number of the lower graded staff, was the least initially supportive towards its introduction. Technology was expected to impact on the working practices of NALGO members more than on those belonging to other unions. Whilst no overt barriers were experienced, any difficulties actually experienced were expected to have been resolved at local workplace level.

A new technology enabling agreement was negotiated with NALGO. It was agreed that new technology should only be introduced after full consultation with those affected by its introduction. The prime responsibility for consultation was agreed as resting with department managers, who were required to inform their staff and the Workplace Representative of plans to introduce technology before it is installed.

It was similarly agreed that within an organization as large as Hampshire County Council it is impractical to control and monitor in detail the introduction of all new technology. Therefore the main purposes of the agreement were to establish procedures for consultation and to safeguard staff in terms of health and safety, training and job protection. The most detailed section of the agreement included a health and safety code of practice. Positioning of terminals, documents, desks and lighting are given detailed recommendations. Hampshire County Council undertakes to meet any reasonable glasses prescription charge for changes in prescription arising from employees' work with screens.

Most consultation and discussion has focused on health and safety implications. Unions were said to have generally supported technology because they understood it to be part of the organizational change which was linked to changes in service provision.

Displaced Workers

The new technology agreement provides assurance that the county is committed to avoiding compulsory redundancy, and contains a number of redeployment provisions. However, some of the reductions in staffing levels originally expected did not take effect. When word processing systems were first introduced in 1977/78 a policy of reducing staff by natural wastage was adopted. But, due to the growth of the organization as a whole, the policy of redeployment and the fact that total employment levels were rising, a few staff who were displaced from their original jobs have been reabsorbed as a result of the overall growth pattern.

Payment Systems

Technology was regarded by Hampshire County Council as an enabling and not a bargaining factor. However, on an individual basis a steady flow of claims was received for regrading due to increased responsibility through the use of computers. The county considers these on their individual merits. If it is agreed that each job does carry additional responsibility then the county are prepared to agree to regrading; they are prepared to pay more if they receive more!

When word processing systems were newly introduced premiums were paid to employees with the relevant skills. Those using the systems were upgraded by one. This practice is now under review as skills which were formerly at a premium can no longer be so regarded. It is part of the general expectation that newly recruited staff will in due course be conversant with basic computer skills.

Personnel Management

Problems experienced which had implications for the personnel and training sections had little to do with lack of technical support or failures in communications regarding the 'conceptual' aspects of information technology. It has not proved possible to date to invest sufficient time and resources in training. The central training section and the training wing of the Information Technology Services section assist departments with their own training needs and with the provision of short practical introductory and more advanced courses. 18 months ago, Office Automation Awareness training was provided for several thousand managers.

The difficulty has been not to gain employees' acceptance of the need for training, but to be able to schedule time in which training can be undertaken. The schools context is expected to present particular difficulties in the future. Finding time to train the half of the county's workforce who are part timers can be difficult. Training in work time takes them away from the job, and on what basis should they be invited to take part in training on a day on which they would not normally be at work?

However, it has been found that these factors have not prevented the county from gaining the benefits from technology. It has taken longer to work towards a significantly robust distributed system than was initially envisaged. But once this is achieved then the full capacity of the technology can be utilized. A number of approaches are being planned to overcome the skills gap. Training is expected to be regarded as a bigger issue in the future. New techniques can be devised to provide training, including the use of the technology itself to deliver the training.

The personnel management system will provide more thorough and sophisticated information, including profiles of training skills and turnover trends. Previously it was not possible to identify such personnel trends, and other useful analytical data. With the development of the personnel systems, departments will have more flexibility in the amount and quality of personnel information available to them. Nonetheless, as most information is now computerized, this could pose problems and raise questions of confidentiality. In the final analysis personnel issues and the handling of them can only be dealt with by people and not machines.

Northern Ireland Electricity

Background (1988)

Established as the Northern Ireland Electricity Service by the Electricity Supply (Northern Ireland) Order 1972, this autonomous body was a new organization created by a merger of the four undertakings then covering Northern Ireland. The main functions of Northern Ireland Electricity (NIE) are to develop economical methods of generating, transmitting and distributing electricity, to secure electrification of rural areas (now virtually complete) and to simplify and standardize methods of charge for electricity.

The Minister of State for Northern Ireland responsible for industrial and economic affairs appoints the members of the Board, consisting of the Chairman, the Deputy Chairman, and not more than seven other members, including a representative of the General Consumer Council for Northern Ireland and a representative of the Trade Union movement.

NIE comprises 11 management units covering Headquarters, six Areas and four Power Stations.

Employees
The total workforce can be divided into four main groups as follows:

Managerial	45
Engineering and Technical	897
Industrial	3,197
Administrative, Clerical & Sales	1,471
Total	5,610 (including trainees)

These four categories identify the four main bargaining groups within NIE. There are four autonomous negotiating bodies which determine terms and conditions of employment for staff as follows:

NI Joint Managerial Committee – managerial staff are
                                                         represented by the Electrical
                                                         Power Engineers' Association
                                                         (EPEA)

NI Join Board   – engineering and technical
                                                         staff are represented by the
                                                         EPEA

NI Joint Industrial Council   – industrial staff are
                                                         represented by EETPU, ATGWU,
                                                         AEU, GMBATU

NI Joint Council   – administrative, clerical and
                                                         sales staff are represented
                                                         by APEX and EETPU (clerical
                                                         section)

The industrial relations machinery replicates the machinery which exists
in the Electricity Supply Industry (ESI) in Great Britain. The main terms
and conditions of NIE employees correspond with those which apply
within the ESI in Great Britain. NIE is not involved directly in the
negotiating processes in the ESI but operates under a policy of parity with
the terms and conditions which exist in the ESI in Great Britain.

NIE is a strongly unionized organization and, as well as the four
main negotiating committees, at the 11 managed units there exist local
staff committees (Manual, Foremen, Technical, Clerical) which deal with
local issues and in the event of failure to agree, submit such disagreements
upwards to their main committee.

Separate from the four negotiating committees there is a consultative structure. The basic purpose of the consultative machinery is to deal
with any matter of mutual interest to management and employees which
falls outside the scope of the negotiating machinery. The aim is to seek to
reach agreement with employees on such matters, but unlike the negotiating structure, matters are not subject to arbitration nor status quo in the
event of disagreements. This structure also differs from the negotiating
structure in that trade union membership of the consultative committees
comprises representatives of the different staff groups sitting together to
discuss matters with NIE management.

The personnel function

The personnel activities under the Personnel Manager comprise a high degree of centralization but the Employee Relations function operates in a somewhat less centralized fashion.

The role of the Employee Relations Department can be stated as:

- Policy, e.g. legislation, parity, organization-wide issues

- Procedures, i.e. that they exist to put into effect the IR policies of NIE

- Standards, i.e. to ensure policies/procedures/agreements operate properly across the organization

- Formal Machinery, i.e. ensuring the machineries are properly serviced and function effectively

- Advice – to management on IR issues so as to assist management in progressing matters throughout the machinery or within procedural agreements

- Representational, i.e. at external tribunals, arbitration or conciliation.

At each Area and Power Station there is an administrative officer who reports to the local manager but in a functional sense represents the personnel activity at local level. Local managers are responsible for their own industrial relations actions locally. They use the central IR Department for advice and guidance in dealing with local issues but may not act outside the national agreements. They are encouraged to view the IR and consultative machineries as a means through which change can be brought about in a unionized environment.

The introduction of technology

The Electricity Supply Industry has always viewed change as an ongoing phenomenon and the adoption of new techniques and modes of working have occurred progressively in a harmonious way. The various joint agreements contain clauses dealing with efficiency and the adoption of new working methods in a co-operative manner and these agreements have been used by management, over the years, as a means for bringing about the greater efficiencies made available by successive advances in technology and working methods.

In examining the way in which the main bargaining groups deal with change, the managerial group can be set to one side since it in fact is the group, on behalf of NIE, involved in initiating change within the other three negotiating bodies.

Comments on the other three negotiating bodies in relation to changing technology are summarized below:

i) *Northern Ireland Joint Board (NIJB)*

This group of staff compromises professional engineering and other technical staff who, as well as having a progressive outlook towards the new technologies and embracing the changes which these bring about, are often those who assist management in introducing new working methods for industrial staff. The main concern of the trade union side of the NIJB has been to ensure that staffing structures and staffing issues arising from changing technology are fully debated before changes take place which might impinge on manning arrangements and practices. As much importance is placed on the informal discussions and procedures as on the formal structures, to ensure that change is fully debated and implemented harmoniously. The trade union side has never sought to extract a price for co-operating in the introduction of technical change, agreeing with management that the most important consideration in this regard is ensuring that the proper rate for the job is paid and that the rate for the job is determined by the level of duties and responsibilities flowing from the changes.

The trade union side of the NIJB has ensured that its members share in new working methods arising from technological change which impinge on the engineering activities of NIE. There has been considerable progress in introducing computer technology within the organization, initially into the financial and administrative functions but more recently impinging upon the engineering and technical activities. The NIJB has been anxious to ensure that systems and development work in this context are not seen as the sole province of NI Joint Council staff. As a consequence, engineering staff represented by the NI Joint Board have been introduced into the computer systems and business systems development departments, working alongside NI Joint Council staff who have traditionally filled systems analysis posts. This move, as well as introducing necessary new skills and experience into the systems function, is also of assistance in maintaining the co-operation of engineering staff whose mode of working is affected by changes in technology.

ii) *Northern Ireland Joint Industrial Council (NIJIC)*

In understanding the way in which technological change is adopted and introduced into the working environment of this group of staff it is necessary to explain some of the background to a significant part of the NIJIC Agreement. The NIJIC adopted in 1980 a new salary structure agreement for industrial staff which, below the level of foreman, assimilated a multitude of job titles and rates of pay into five broad bands. Main duties summaries (MDSs) were prepared for the many and various industrial jobs, the appropriate banding for each main duties summary was agreed and MDSs allocated to one of the five bands. As well as rationalizing what had previously been a piecemeal situation of job titles and job rates, it also created a situation whereby better control could be exercised over the process of determining the proper rate for the job.

Another important factor of this agreement was the clause dealing with future changes. It is under the procedures set out in this clause that change is introduced by management into the industrial staff arena which, added to the agreements on co-operation and efficiency, have enabled change to be introduced in a harmonious and systematic way embracing a consultative approach by management.

Jobs continue to be graded on the basis of duties and responsibilities as provided for by the NIJIC Agreement with no serious pressure being exerted for special rates to be created in return for acceptance of new working practices arising from technical change. There is no new technology-type agreement; the thrust of the NIJIC Agreement is towards the recognition that change is an ongoing process regardless of the reasons which cause the change, e.g. new technology, and the obligation for staff to adopt new modes of working subject to consultation has been enshrined in and reinforced by successive annual pay settlements.

iii) *Northern Ireland Joint Council (NIJC)*

The joint agreement for this group of staff contains a new technology agreement. It forms part of clauses dealing with efficiency and co-operation and is intended to complement the role of the negotiating machinery and local consultative arrangements. It is accepted that it is the responsibility of management operating through the normal procedures of consultation with the trade unions to improve the organization's methods, work norms or objectives, machinery and equipment and job content.

The code requires that when management proposes to introduce 'automated and new equipment' the fullest prior consultation with employees and their representatives will take place. The code also identifies those new technology matters on which consultation should take place as being:

a)   the breadth of operation contemplated and its benefits

b)   manning levels as determined by recognized measurement and
     control procedures

c)   effect on the level of duties and responsibilities

d)   training and re-training

e)   ergonomics

f)   health and safety.

As far as computer technology is concerned, the group of staff most
affected is NIJC staff and a number of difficulties have been experienced
when proposals have been presented for the introduction of new office
technology.

Employee Commitment

It will be clear from what already has been said that the joint agreements
require management to consult on the impact of changing technology and
staff expect this consultation to take place fully. Detailed procedures have
been prepared as a guide for management in dealing with their responsibilities to consult with their staff and with the representatives of staff.

In the context of employee commitment, the initiatives which management have recently begun to improve employee communication are
worth reporting. An attitude survey has been completed aimed at establish-
ing the views of staff towards such issues as the degree to which staff wish
to be informed and consulted on decisions which affect them, and also how
they perceive NIE's management style. Work continues in analyzing the
results and identifying the actions which the results indicate as being
appropriate. Both the survey and the analysis and identification of actions
have been carried out on a joint management/staff communication process. Team briefing has been introduced on a pilot basis with the intention
that it would be extended to other management units in due course. A programme of team building is also under way which involves employees
from management down to foremen level.

Consideration is also being given to the organizational structure of
NIE, not only for the purpose of ensuring that the business objectives are
being best served by the structure as it currently stands, but also to ensure

that the structure enables the efficient flow of upward and downward communications.

The trade union officials within the industry have always operated an effective communication system with their members and at times it has appeared that the trade unions have been the communicators of management's message. This is a situation not untypical in a large unionized organization and management's efforts to improve its communication with staff might be perceived by the trade unions as a device for undermining their position. In fact its real purpose arises from the fact that management believe that to win commitment they must improve, amongst other things, communication between management, supervision and the workforce.

Trade Union Reactions

In discussions with the NIJC, much attention has been focused on grading issues with the trade union side, sometimes giving the impression that regrading should be the automatic consequence of their acceptance of new technology. When the NIJC new technology agreement was adopted, a review of clerical grades also took place and a number of new grading levels were created. Whilst it was the intention that these would be allocated on the basis of duties and responsibilities, there has been pressure to concede the application of these grades in return for co-operation in technical change. The arguments involved have taken a number of different forms including the assertion that working with the new equipment necessarily involved a higher level of skill. From the management viewpoint this was not always the case and, in some instances, the reverse was more accurate. There were occasions when, because grading matters had not been agreed at the consultative stage, prior to the acceptance of new technology the trade union side in effect were applying a veto on management's proposals. Later agreements augmenting the new technology agreements made it clear that this sort of veto was not appropriate and in cases where gradings were not agreed, such disagreements would be referred to a separate procedure for resolution while the consultation leading to the introduction of management's proposals would proceed separately. This has assisted the process of getting change implemented but what seems to have emerged is that the clerical unions are now paying closer attention to the job grading criteria, for if the criteria can be changed, higher grades might be possible.

The agreement also requires management to apply appropriate techniques in determining manning levels, thus requiring additional resources to be allocated to the process of job measurement so that such issues could be dealt with as required by the consultative arrangements. So as to maintain the confidence of staff, management agreed to second into the management services unit lay representatives of the trade unions, to carry out the measurement exercise under management's supervision. The secondees were selected by a joint management/trade union interview panel, are broadly representative of the diverse clerical activities of NIE, and were trained in the application of the particular measurement technique.

More recently, the trade union side have focused their attention on health, safety and ergonomic issues. The health and safety standards to be observed when new technology is introduced into the office situation in NIE are based upon Health and Safety Executive Guidelines which are endorsed by the Industry through its Health and Safety Committee (HESAC). The NI HESAC equivalent has adopted these ESI standards and seeks to ensure that they apply whenever new technology and VDUs are introduced.

More and more attention is being paid by the trade union side to observance of these standards, but since much of the office accommodation was designed in a pre office technology era, it is sometimes necessary to compromise between what is desirable and what is possible. This has led to management undertaking a review of office accommodation and assessing its adequacy in the light of these new technology requirements.

The trade union side has also been alerted to the many forms of research which have been carried out concerning possible health and safety hazards arising from new technology in the office. Matters including eye strain, backache, skin disorders and the dangers of radiation for female staff, especially pregnant staff, have been raised with management. The trade unions have also sought to conduct their own survey within the organization to establish the views of their members on a range of new technology health and safety matters. The survey has not taken place but a joint sub-committee has been established to investigate new technology applications in the office to see how they would measure up to the HESAC guidelines referred to earlier.

The trade unions have played a valuable part in setting and maintaining proper standards in this regard. Management accepts that the trade unions have every right to ensure that the health of their members is protected. Management is anxious to provide a safe working environment and is happy with a collaborative approach in identifying problem areas and ensuring that proper standards apply.

Personnel Management

As previously mentioned, line management is encouraged to view the negotiating and consultative structure as a vehicle for winning the co-operation of staff in bringing about change. The various joint agreements require management to consult with staff on the introduction of new working arrangements and consequently, the more change that is required the more management is required to consult with members of staff. The role of the personnel function, therefore, has been to ensure that management locally consult properly, at the right times with the necessary information. Many of the difficulties which have been experienced have not been so much concerned with the changes themselves, but with the way management has sought to introduce change either by not consulting adequately or by not beginning the consultative process at a sufficiently early stage. Consequently, personnel centrally monitor the progress of major change proposals through the various stages of the consultative procedures.

Both the speed of change and the impact on staff have required greater consideration to be given to the means for resolving the effects of such change on staff and staff numbers. The view is taken that it is unlikely that staff's co-operation will be forthcoming if proposals which are likely to affect their jobs are not also accompanied by proposals for dealing with the associated personnel problems. A range of policies have been developed to deal with the personnel implications of major change proposals. These include:

- a policy of no enforced redundancy (subject to the co-operation of staff)

- retraining and redeployment

- personal salary protection arrangements

- voluntary selective severance arrangements

- part-time working and temporary employment.

These measures have required greater emphasis to be placed upon manpower planning in terms of quantifying requirements on a geographical and on a skills basis, identifying changes anticipated in the composition of the workforce, adjusting recruitment plans accordingly and seeking by retraining and counselling to rematch manpower to workload across the organization in as humane a way as possible. This task is not made easier if staff are comparatively unwilling to move geographically. To counter this, attention is being paid to the need for staff to work flexibly, for if staff cannot be geographically redeployed to the same job, redeployment could take place within their own managed unit if flexibility between jobs was improved.

The major changes which are now possible through new technology are having a gradual effect on the structure of the organization, which in turn has significant implications for the personnel function. Firstly, personnel is becoming more involved at the early stages of planning. It is more noticeable that the personnel function acts more in anticipation of change occurring in preparing training plans, quantifying changes in the nature of work and the number of posts. This requires a closer relationship on the one hand between those responsible for organization planning and on the other hand, those responsible for the planning of the new systems, since the latter are seen as the mainspring of future change. Secondly, line management needs to be better equipped to handle the introduction of change and to win acceptance of their proposals. This raises questions of the management style appropriate to securing co-operation, and the re-cruitment, selection and training of supervisors and managers who can handle this role.

Swansea City Council

Background (1988)

Swansea City Council provides a range of public services to a population of 187,400. 84 per cent live in the urban area of Swansea. The remaining 16 per cent live in a large rural area to one side of the city.

The departments of the council include the Housing Department which lets and collects rents from 20,000 properties. The council also owns and operates 33 sheltered homes. As the largest land owner in the area, the council has its own estate agency. Its building company provides maintenance and repair services for 20,000 council properties.

The Development Department employs architects and quantity surveyors in the specification, design and maintenance of buildings. Services from this Department also include town and country planning. The City Engineer's Department has responsibility for highway maintenance, street lighting, drainage and sewers. Refuse collection and disposal are a co-ordinated service provided by the Council.

The Chief Environmental Health Officer has responsibilities which include building control. These can be for new buildings or for changes to existing property. Improvement grants are controlled by this department.

The Municipal Director of Music has responsibility for the Swansea Festival, which is a major cultural event in Wales. The Grand Theatre, the Art Gallery and Museum, and the Archives Section are included in the cultural and leisure services provided by the Council. The City Leisure Centre, the international running track and swimming pools are maintained by the Sports and Recreation Department.

The Administrative Department, the City Treasurer, and the Information Technology Department provide services for the operation of the City Council itself. The Chief Executive's Department provides legal services to the authority and secretarial services to the council and for its civic functions.

The activities of the council are divided between three main operating units. The Guildhall in Swansea City Centre is the major administrative unit and all departments, with one exception, are located on this site. The Building Department is located separately. Community Programme and Youth Training operations are housed in a centralized unit.

Employees

Swansea City Council employs 3,100 individuals. 1,000 are white collar staff, 1,300 are permanent blue collar and the remaining 800 are employed on short term employment measures. These include the Community Programme projects and the Youth Training Scheme. Annual turnover revenue is about £42 million and annual expenditure on capital is £20 million.

Of the white collar staff 30 are top managers, 224 are senior managers, 229 are middle managers and 500 are clerical and technical staff. This workforce is totally unionized. A significant majority are members of NALGO, whilst others are either members of NUPE or FUMPO. (The Federation of Unions and Managers and Professional Officers represents chief officers.)

Of 400 people in the Building Department, 200 are UCATT members, 80 are members of the EETPU and the remainder are TGWU members. In the Central Repair Depot 15 belong to AEU. Three printshop employees are members of the NGA and SOGAT '83. 280 belong to NUPE and the majority of the remainder to the TGWU, but with two belonging to GMBATU. Of 280 staff working in parks and open spaces, 50 per cent are NUPE workers. Amongst municipal theatre staff 40 belong to BETA.

Pay bargaining is conducted nationally for all staff except those who are members of BETA. For theatre staff there is a locally bargained agreement. However, bargaining conditions for all other staff are such that a new flexibility is being introduced into the national agreements which will soon be open to local interpretation. Most flexibility at local level is found in settlements for weekend, shift and overtime working. For example, four additional days holiday have been negotiated for employees to be taken after a Bank Holiday.

The personnel function

Swansea City Council employs a principle personnel officer, a senior personnel officer, three personnel assistants and three personnel clerks.

The personnel function operates on the principle that all personnel professionals will be employed in undertaking what could be described as the same job. All are involved in white and blue collar recruitment. Equally all are involved in the monitoring and control of absence, counselling and control of probationary periods. The personnel committee of the council meets monthly and decisions are actioned against the names of individuals on the day. Whilst all personnel officers are involved in employee relations at shop steward level, the two most senior officers are involved at union district officer level.

The introduction of technology

Information technology has had the widest application and impact on staff at Swansea City Council. Most employees of the council understand 'computers' to be synonymous with 'technology' in the contexts in which they work. Most of the repercussions have been for white collar and managerial staff. However, the introduction of a computer to monitor blue collar staff working practices at the Central Repair Vehicle Depot had significant implications for Depot organization and manning levels.

Until very recently Swansea City Council was part of a local authority consortium which was led by a different authority. The consortium operated a central computer unit with an ICL mainframe computer. Changes occurred which indicated that on grounds of cost Swansea City Council would not be justified in continuing its membership. The decision was made to phase in an IBM mainframe system over which the council would have total control of access and costs. Also planned was a considerable lead-in time in order to allow adjustment for staff duties and training.

The IBM system installed is a 38 system mainframe. There is also an IBM system 36 function. The distributed facilities of the mainframe are all from the 38 system. Facilities are distributed widely through the departments of the council, although not all of the facilities are yet in operation. However, all secretaries employed by the council have now been supplied with personal computers and can be part of the distributed facilities of the mainframe computers. Facilities include a range of mini and micro desk top computers in addition to the mainframe terminals.

Computer systems were planned to be introduced into departmental systems on a phased programme. The most clear cut application was perceived to be in the Treasurer's Department. Finance and accountancy systems were seen to be most susceptible to change. The major technical difficulty experienced was that very few standard software packages were available for the new IBM system. As a result staff had to adapt to new software.

Over the first year of development of the range of computer functions, 1986, 300 personal computers were introduced. During the course of 1987 it was anticipated that a further 300 would be introduced. As the whole system develops over the next few years it is expected that further applications will be developed. Most significant amongst these is expected to be a form of budgetry profiling and monitoring. Future personnel applications could include monitoring of labour turnover, wage drift, and attendance levels. Such overall closer control of manpower statistics could provide line managers with information not previously as accessible.

The personnel department has no direct access to the mainframe computer. However, it has use of a dedicated stand alone system which computes council employees' flexitime details, holidays and sickness.

The efficiency of public service information systems has been improved by the information technology programme. The Centre for Trade and Industry operates an information system which was amongst the first of its kind in the country. Members of the public can key-in their own requirements for theatre tickets, hotel bookings and 'What's On' information generally. In addition, the effect of the total computerization of the Housing Benefits section means a considerable increase in the speed with which public queries and payments can be dealt.

The council considers that its secretarial services have been up-graded to a very considerable degree as a direct result of new technology. Photocopiers with their own collators have been introduced into the Copying Room for example. Such machines have helped to cut the hours of staff time that would formerly have been spent on such simple but lengthy operations.

Organizational Change

The Treasurer and the Director of Administration agreed a key personnel strategy to deal with the manpower requirements generated by the technology. The main policy was to take people with the expertise and teach them how to train. Supernumerary posts were created at a senior level. A supernumerary section of three, in addition to the Assistant Treasurers, 'sorted out the nuts and bolts'. The fact that there was little difficulty experienced with the introduction of the 'major' system was attributed to the strategy of removing people with expertise from their original jobs, whilst giving them the brief to help design the system and to groom each department in changes in working practices.

Prior to computerization the Organization and Methods section consisted of five employees led by an individual with computer expertise. During computerization the Organization and Methods section evolved into the Information Technology Department employing 20 people. 15 entirely new posts were created. In addition the post of Information Technology Manager was created. Two development teams were put in control of a computer development programme until 1988. One 'problem solver' has been deployed to move around the council on a peripatetic basis to investigate individual problems.

The Central Repair Vehicle Depot had been of concern to senior management for some time. A computer system was introduced with the help of Management Services to monitor all aspects including working practices. As a result of new information on working practices and costs, decisions were taken to reduce staff costs and cut the spares bill. In twelve months the Depot was 'turned around' and is now on a sound financial footing.

Employee reactions

Employees generally were perceived to be more than ready to gain 'hands on' keyboard experience. The view of union representatives and employees diverged at a number of stages. The first Procedural Agreement on the Introduction of New Technology fell into disuse because the procedural requirements were upstaged by, on the one hand, the enthusiasm of white collar staff to use the new equipment, and on the other, by the willingness of senior council executives to introduce the equipment.

Despite and perhaps because of such willingness to proceed, a 'skill gap' was quickly identified. A single training officer reports to the Director of Administration. Initially this role was a co-ordinating one; it had proved extremely difficult to recruit training expertise to cope with the demand for training for the hundreds of employees who have contact with computers. Thus, although the 'major' systems were introduced without major difficulty, the operation of the 'minor' systems was slowed by the lack of resources to meet the 'skills gap'.

Implications for the personnel function

The impact on personnel management roles was seen as one of creating the
environment into which technology could be successfully introduced. In
order to achieve this the Management Services section and the Personnel
Section were encouraged to dissolve some of the barriers which had
previously determined their division of labour. The new approach was to
be in multi-disciplinary terms. The previous 'departmental ethos' was
encouraged to give way to a co-ordinated role for all administrative
functions including Organization and Methods, Work Study and
Personnel.

Employee Commitment

The first agreement on the introduction of new technology was signed in
May 1982. This specified fairly detailed procedural requirements to be
followed for the purposes of consultation. At normal monthly meetings,
attended by council executives, the organization and methods manager
and two or three shop stewards or representatives from each department,
a resumé of the up to date position on new technology was to be discussed.
Details of new proposals were to be included in the discussions. Minutes
of the meetings were to include the estimated cost benefit to the authority.
There was provision for follow-up consultation and additional meetings
once representatives had consulted their members.

In practice this agreement was found to be weighted too much
towards procedures. Too much work was involved for representatives and
the personnel department alike, and the pace of change overtook the pace
of time it took to operate the procedures. Apart from some health and safety
considerations, and some consequent adjustment of the length of time to
be spent on VDU work without breaks, employees themselves had no
major reservations about the changes in working practices. The monthly
meetings fell into disuse.

Under the second (and current) agreement it is agreed that normal
consultation processes will not be invoked when a change from a manual
system to a computerized system is made, or when one system is replaced
by another. However, consultation will be followed where substantial or
significant changes are likely to occur that are fundamental to the nature
of the work and the organization.

Since the demise of the first agreement and its replacement by the
current agreement, signed in April 1983, the personnel department has had

minimal involvement. Previously personnel staff were occupied in servicing the meetings and undertaking the cost benefit calculations.

Trade Union Reactions

The union's initial claim that all individuals working with new technology should be awarded significant pay increases changed through the course of negotiations into agreement on principle that there should be global benefits for the employees of the authority as a whole. A central union fund was set up from which the union could distribute funds to benefit employees (subject to the authority of the council). Latterly, however, the authority has made specific suggestions as to how these funds should be distributed. In the second agreement the central fund was swept away and the authority agreed to finance the salary of a full time secretary. A lump sum payment subject to annual revision was agreed for updating their equipment, children's Christmas party, education 'schools' and meetings convened by NALGO. In exchange the union side agreed to accept all new technology until 1985 (September).

The main agreement has not to date been amended further. In exchange for the acceptance of all new technology, the authority enhanced the holiday allowances of those graded on the lowest points of their spinal scales. Two additional days were added to their annual entitlement and one day was added to the entitlement of those graded nearer the top of their scales. There were also improvements for those entitled to long service leave. These holiday improvements were not part of the union side claim. Section 5 of the terms of agreement states that the authority will have the discretion to introduce new technology, or update existing technology, as the demands of the service may require in exchange for these specific improvements.

Many initial union claims never became, or are not currently, negotiating issues. However, the union side were insistent upon the inclusion of certain provisions within the agreements. These included health and safety provisions in particular and these are fairly extensive within the current agreement. The union could currently be described as co-operative to the introduction of technology whilst retaining certain specific requirements on how it should be operated. Also retained is the mandatory use of consultation procedures in the event of fundamental changes affecting jobs, working practices and the organization as a whole.

Displaced Workers

Taking into account all the employees of Swansea City Council, almost a quarter (22 per cent) are aged over 50. At the end of 1986 the authority brought a voluntary retirement scheme into operation. Under this scheme a proportion of employees over 55 left the service of the council. No younger members of the workforce were displaced as a result of the introduction of technology, and the introduction of the voluntary retirement scheme was motivated at least as much by competitive tendering considerations as by change which came about as a result of technology.

Whilst no white collar employees were directly displaced as a result of technology, certain blue collar employees in the Vehicle Repair Depot were retired early on individual schemes under the provisions of the Local Government Superannuation Act. This was implemented as a direct result of the monitoring of working practices by new technology.

The current agreement contains some specific provisions for training. It is stated that all employees who require it will have access to training for use of technology. Employees due for promotion will similarly receive training to enable them to be promoted, and no employee who is due for promotion will be debarred on the grounds that he or she has no experience of technology.

Such provisions place an additional workload on trainers. Swansea City Council employs one Training Officer and two Health and Safety Officers in the Administration Department. During the initial phases of technical change the training function was confined to an overall co-ordinating role with an emphasis on some individual 'fault finding' and 'problem solving'. Early training initiatives addressed essential areas of work.

At the request of a computer 'User Group' and the management team, an investigation of training provision was conducted. New in-house training provision will consequently range between introductory courses for new but regular users of new technology, courses providing users with the opportunity to develop their own systems on the IBM system 38, and courses for the effective operation of personal computers, word processors, supercalc, and databases.

Payment Systems

In the first (procedural) agreement the principle was established that any cost benefit arising from the introduction of new technology would be shared on a mutually agreed basis. Initially, the unions (principally NALGO) argued for a list of items including salary improvements of £600 per person and increased holiday allowances. However, the authority were not prepared to negotiate on pay generally as a union condition for working with technology. Despite one early exception in which typing/secretarial staff were regraded, the authority did not wish this to be established as a precedent. A section to this effect is clearly stated in the second agreement ('On the use of New Technology'): 'Direct involvement with new technology will not, of itself, justify a salary regrading'. Provisions were retained for cases where an individual's job had been changed beyond recognition by the use of substantial new skills, although this was an unusual event in the authority as a whole.

Prior to technology making a full impact on the secretarial services of the council, employees in the typing pool were the only group of employees who worked on a productivity and bonus basis. The single criteria to which the bonuses were related was speed. With the introduction of technology this criteria has no relevance at all as a measurement of working practices. The decision was made to remove all productivity payments and a regrading programme was implemented. Each individual working on computers was moved up one grade. The authority maintained that this was the first and last time that regrading would be undertaken. The union side have not backed a claim for regrading and/or more pay for other employees working directly with other computers.

Thirty different shiftwork patterns were already established and there has been no change to these patterns as a result of staff working with technology. The new computer staff recently recruited are employed on established shifts.

Personnel Management

The major impact of technical change for the personnel section has been in terms of administrative improvements in their own information systems. Most of the work involved with breaking the new computerized record keeping methods has been undertaken by the three personnel clerks.

Under the leadership of the former director of administration, employees operated in conditions under which there was a fairly strict division of labour between the personnel section and the management services section. The consequence of the different management style of the new director has meant that a new emphasis is placed on dissolving the inherited barriers between these two groups, and on a new flexibility in the division of labour between the personnel officers themselves. Although this had been due to the influence of a new management style rather than as a result of the impact of technology on the organization, such new flexibility in working practices was thought to ease the path of technology into the organization.

Postscript
Subsequent to this case study having been written, a major reorganization has been taking place within the council and the departmental structure in the future is to be different from that which is included here.

BOC Transhield

Background (May 1989)

As one of the subsidiary distribution service companies of the industrial gases group BOC Ltd, BOC Transhield provides a 'fresh and chill' food warehousing and distribution service to Marks and Spencers' stores throughout the UK and Europe. Marks and Spencers is BOC Transhield's single customer and the company delivers food products to 234 retail stores.

The company has achieved a steady growth rate per annum and the depots at Crewe and Thatcham have opened since the early 1980s contributing to the company's annual turnover of some £60 million.

Employees

BOC Transhield employs 1,647 at seven regional depots and headquarters in Guildford. The most numerically significant sectors of the workforce are warehouse operatives and drivers. Remaining employees are divided between managers, supervisors, administrative, clerical, catering and hygiene staff.

A post entry closed shop was agreed at the time of the start up of the company in 1970. A close relationship is maintained with the TGWU. Staff below management levels are members of the union's white collar section, ACTSS. Bargaining on pay and conditions is conducted at company level with wage deals in recent years covering two years at a time.

The personnel function

Personnel managers each have personnel responsibility for two depots. They report to the site general manager and are assisted by a personnel officer. This team have responsibility for first and second stage recruitment, induction, depot industrial relations and the company's communication programme.

The company level personnel team include the Assistant Managing Director, who is in effect the Personnel Director, the General Manager Personnel and Training, a Human Resources Manager, Head Office Personnel Manager, Recruitment and Training Manager, Training and Communications Manager, a Hygiene and Safety Manager and an Industrial Relations Liaison Officer.

The introduction of technology

BOC Transhield's operations have benefited from the step by step assimilation of certain technological improvements. Some changes could be described as arising from low level technical improvements. Thinner walled trailer vehicles mean that vehicles can carry larger loads. The design of draw bar vehicles means that two trailers can be used as one vehicle, thus reducing the number of outward and return 'runs' required for larger loads. Roll pallets and power pallet trucks contribute to a faster turnaround of produce in the warehouses.

Information technology has had a considerable impact in the operations office. Here liaison is carried out with Marks and Spencer's Baker Street operation. A proof of delivery system and priority delivery system (PDS) have been introduced in the last 3 years. Additionally, a pilot electronic point of sale system means that information can be fed through the phone network. The further co-ordination of BOC Transhield's and Marks and Spencer's information systems is a matter for continuing planning and discussion.

Other technical improvements include the introduction of micro computers for traffic planning. The use of micros for labour utilization planning is expected to have implications for improved management control in the future. The company is also examining the possibilities of the introduction of computerized personnel systems.

Organizational Change

New systems introduced into the operations office have meant a restructuring of work allocation and the creation of some entirely new jobs. The job content of operations planners' jobs has changed to include more data handling areas. In addition, the centralization of all keying functions and the use of new software meant that clerical and calculation work was removed from their normal workload.

The post of operations administrative manager was created as an entirely new post, as were posts of team leaders and PDS clerks. The clerks liaise with stores and input from one system to another. Selected operations planners were promoted into the positions of team leaders. The operations planners' responsibilities include checking input against stock levels, and the production of instructions to enable the warehouse to allocate stocks to individual stores.

Some shift pattern changes at depot level were necessitated by the new technology. Whilst this entailed a slight loss of earnings the preparedness of employees to accept these flexibility requirements was felt to be one of the benefits of an open and strong relationship with the TGWU. Because employees have been able to understand the nature of Transhield's business they are able to accept that organizational changes are a result of the exclusive relationship with the company's key customer and their business needs.

The early developments of computer technology were applied, as in most businesses, to payroll, costing and other financial information. Continuing development has now allowed the provision of more management information of higher quality sooner. The opportunity now exists for a totally integrated system which would include personnel, payroll and finance.

Employee Commitment

In 1974 the company launched a Human Relations Charter. This embodied a number of principles and emphasized the importance of two-way communication. The appropriate constitutional framework was established in the form of national and local consultative committees. Terms and conditions of work are negotiated at national level. Matters discussed of mutual interest to management and employee representatives at local level could include the local application of terms and conditions, training and educational activities.

Although time has brought some pressure to bear upon the principles formulated in the Charter in the early 1970s, the consultative frameworks continue to be regarded as extremely important in the context of the continuing principle of an open style of communications.

A Working Party of the National Joint Negotiating Committee was specially formed to deal with the changes affecting both operational and equipment planners.

Trade Union Reactions

From the time of the company's start up, BOC Transhield took the view
that single union representation was the most beneficial route to establish
good company and workforce relationships and to avoid the problems of
multi unionism. Transhield feel that there has been mutual benefit from
this relationship. This understanding allowed the company to introduce
technology as and when the business required it by following the normal
consultation procedures. In this context a formal technology agreement
was thought to be inappropriate.

The most recently opened depot is at Thatcham where new work
practices were installed and is thus regarded as being at the forefront of
change. Consequently, operating flexibility is more marked here than at
other depots. For example, the drivers based at Thatcham were the first
group of drivers to undertake some work in the warehouse.

These flexibility factors at Thatcham have led to the recognition that
working practices at other depots do not fully meet the requirements of a
progressive warehousing and distribution company. Whilst the introduction of these new work practices at other depots placed relationships under
some stress these difficulties have been overcome.

Displaced Workers

As a result of technical change the equipment planners occupied an
organizational vacuum when their jobs effectively disappeared. They
were offered a number of options including redeployment to the warehouse on a charge hand basis but with a compensating lump sum, or
voluntary redundancy.

Because of the expected changes in the technical systems, PDS
clerks are employed on short term contracts. During their first year they
benefit from the same terms and conditions as other employees with the
exception of the company pension scheme. It is agreed that after one year's
service these employees must be considered for permanent status or their
contract concluded. The company has generally been pleased with their
standards and these groups thereby become entitled to permanent status
and eligible for the company pension scheme.

Personnel Management

Technical change has focused attention on a number of recruitment, training and management style issues.

The new skills of managers must include the ability to 'manage by data'. Previously, information about the company operations could be gained from a variety of first hand and paper sources. Currently, much necessary information is available as computer data. In addition, managers' job specifications require that they be flexible, adaptable and good communicators.

These new skill requirements have focused attention on the recruitment requirements for high quality graduates to enter management posts. They are also required to be more numerate than previously, although the qualities of adaptability and flexibility are equally as important. However, this does not mean that personnel policy will necessarily place more emphasis on graduate recruitment for all future management posts. A long standing policy of employee development means that non graduates with the appropriate skills have no less opportunity for a successful management career.

Concluding Comment

The changes made have enabled BOC Transhield to improve its service to the customer, and have placed the company in a stronger position to deal with the challenges of the 1990s. BOC Transhield's human and industrial relations continue to be stable and sound.

Postscript
The above identifies the progress of BOC Transhield Ltd until the end of 1988. Since then BOC Distribution Services has been created with BOC Transhield Ltd forming the major part. Appropriate management and organizational changes have taken place to reflect divisional needs.

Sainsbury's (Retail Division)

Background (May 1989)

Sainsbury's is a leading UK food retailer operating through 280 supermarkets and with just over a 10 per cent share of the UK food and drink market. The retail sector is the fastest growing sector of the economy. Sainsbury's is the largest butcher, wine, fresh fruit and vegetable retailer in the UK. Own brand lines account for over 50 per cent of retail business. Within this very large retail division between 15 and 20 new stores are opened each year.

The distribution market has four large company depots and 30 satellite distribution centres. Sainsbury's also has four associate and five subsidiary companies, including investment companies. Sainsbury's jointly own Haverhill Meat Products with Canada Packer meat processing company and the Homebase home and garden improvement centres with GB-Inno-BM, S.A. SavaCentre and Shaws Supermarkets Inc. in the United States are wholly owned subsidiaries.

Employees

The Sainsbury's Group employs over 90,000 staff of whom 66,500 are employed in the retail branches. Company growth has meant the creation of 19,000 jobs within the last five years. Overall, over 60 per cent of all employees are part time.

Between 3,000 and 4,000 employees work within the distribution network. A further 2,500 are employed at Headquarters centres in Blackfriars and Streatham in central functions such as finance and personnel, and in such roles as buyers, architects, estate managers and food technologists.

Under a new structure implemented in 1988 a store manager has three deputies; a services, administration and reception manager; a fresh foods manager; and a dry goods manager. Some larger stores have up to

30 managers in total, including deputies, depending on the size of the store.

The retail division has a union membership density (USDAW and TGWU) of under seven per cent. Neither salaries nor terms and conditions are negotiated with the unions, although the company does undertake annual consultation.

A post entry closed shop agreement for all employees characterizes the very different, strong and traditional union presence within the distribution division. All pay and conditions of service are determined by annual negotiation with USDAW, TGWU and craft unions including AEU.

The personnel function

The corporate personnel function's responsibilities include manpower resources, training and development and remuneration and benefits, with line personnel managers having responsibility for the main operating divisions of the company, i.e. Retail, Depots, Trading and Central Departments.

The retail division has five area offices each led by an area director with responsibility for around 55 stores. Five personnel managers have area responsibility whilst each retail branch has a personnel manager who is supplemented by a personnel assistant in larger stores.

Using new technology

Sainsbury's is continuing to extend its use of new technology to improve efficiency and give customers better service. To the customer, the most obvious change has been the switch at the checkouts from electronic cash registers to scanning. Now about 80 per cent of stores have scanning equipment.

Surveys have shown that customers appreciated faster service at the tills, the clear and informative receipt, and the more convenient arrangements for the purchase of produce. With scanning information available at head office, buying departments can track the movement of new products, measure the impact of special promotions, and react very quickly to seasonal or unexpected demands. The cumulative effect of these programmes has given the company's retail management a very substantial lead in experience and confidence in the use of computer systems in retail operations.

The new investment has not been exclusively in the branches. A third computer site is just one aspect of much development which has taken place away from the public eye, to give Sainsbury's one of the most advanced warehousing, ordering and delivery systems of any retailer. The efficiency of the delivery system has been significantly increased by totally integrated computerized ordering and the introduction of a new fleet of double decker lorries, each equipped to handle 72 pallets and capable of rapid loading and unloading. The ordering system links branches with buyers and depots to give shorter delivery times and much better control over stock positions as well as very significant savings in management time.

At head office a new micro-computer system has streamlined the merchandizing of products in stores. Known appropriately as Spaceman, it enables available shelf space to be planned graphically on screen, using colours and shapes to make up the most effective shelf allocation for a given store, based both on available space and the ordering and delivery cycle.

In 1987, Sainsbury's took another important step forward with the trial of a full-scale electronic funds transfer at the point of sale (EFTPOS). The trial has proved successful and customers clearly appreciate the speed and ease of EFTPOS transactions. This project has supported Sainsbury's belief that customers will welcome EFTPOS, and the company looks forward to playing its part in the development of a national system.

Over the last five years Sainsbury's computer power has grown at a rate of around 50 per cent a year. One of the most significant developments has been the installation of computers in stores. Today, the process of installing computers in all Sainsbury's stores is almost complete; 285 branches have immediate information for their ordering, stock control, and space allocation. In addition, all stores are connected through a communications network to head office, which enables them to use corporate systems directly; this has brought further improvements to efficiency.

Organizational Change

As the retail market is a very competitive and fast expanding one, a key way forward for Sainsbury's is seen in terms of customer service innovation. Customer services training encourages staff to consider the ways in which they are perceived by the customer. This training in conjunction with the speed and efficiency benefits from laser scanning can equally contribute to the company's maintenance of its competitive position.

The sales assistant's job is now centred on ensuring that each item has been scanned at the purchase point. However, the very nature of the speed and efficiency benefits of this system means that there is a requirement for more packers to help the customers with their purchases, and it is noticeable that cashiers now have slightly more time to communicate with customers, helped by the fact that the new technique requires the cashier to sit facing the customer.

Scanning, together with in-store computing, provide store managers with greater variety and sophistication of information. This can tend to place the accuracy of managers' decisions in the spotlight because much key information is in the form of computer data which is also available to central managers.

Overall, technology has helped improve productivity and has also helped to generate new trade through the stores.

Employee reactions

In general terms employees with operating contact with laser scanning responded positively to the changes in working practices. The advantages of being able to face the customer and the lesser need to use awkward body movements at the checkout position were quickly grasped. Some older employees were less receptive to changes but in many cases management were of the view that these employees were also less dexterous with the old system; the new system simply highlights this and provides further evidence to confirm it. Younger employees were also found to adapt very well to in-store computing and consequently the majority of employees filling systems clerks positions tend to be young, but in these office areas it is also noticeable that older, well established workers have adapted well to the new technology and appreciate the greater involvement and direction which they have.

Employee Commitment

There has been some recognition that the company is practised at communicating in the sense of sending information 'down' the company, but that less emphasis was placed until recently on retrieving information 'back up' the organization. However, within the framework of the Company Programme employees are encouraged to let their views be known to management.

Trade Union Reactions

There is a relatively low level of union strength in branches, usually less than seven per cent of employees. However, union representatives have highlighted the perceived de-merits in the scanning technology. One set of data provided by scanning produces information on individual operator's performance.

Displaced Employees

Sainsbury's does have a redeployment policy, but job displacement from any source has to be seen in the context of company growth and the annual opening of new stores. In addition, it has been found that the adoption of some technology actually creates opportunities. The use of word processors for example means that new forms of information can be made available.

Payment Systems

There has been no regrading as a direct result of technical change in the retail sector. The effect of the technical change is seen as being *volume* related in the sense that the benefits in terms of speed and efficiency mean greater volumes can be, and are, catered for at checkouts. Therefore jobs are not subject to the sort of substantial change which would make them warrant regrading.

Through the company's Profit Sharing and Share Option Schemes nearly a third of employees have a share in Sainsbury's, accounting for around 30 per cent of all the company shareholders.

Personnel Management

Education and training at all levels continue to be the focus for very substantial investment. The high quality of in-company staff training was praised in a report by Dr Paul Johnson, a member of Her Majesty's Inspectorate, who, at Sainsbury's invitation, spent six months studying the company's training programmes. The report, 'Education and Training at Sainsbury's' suggests that Sainsbury's training programmes have many lessons for colleges of further education.

High among priorities has been training in the use of branch computers and the new checkout scanning equipment; 25,000 staff were trained within a very tight time scale. Computer-based training is being used in a variety of ways and has been accepted enthusiastically by staff. This new method of training at the work place is being increasingly relied upon.

The balance of activities remains weighted towards recruitment (especially in labour shortage areas such as the South East), but with training emerging as the activity through which new progress is to be made.

At branch level three or four people report to the branch personnel manager who has responsibility to ensure training planning, co-ordination and execution.

Around 15,000 people were trained on the laser scanning equipment within a year. Training begins with an initial tape slide presentation and interactive video. Thereafter experience is gained at first hand on the shopfloor.

Technology has itself opened up new training techniques. Computer training and systems learning is carried out by distance learning and by self-paced learning where trainees control their own pace through the programme.

Security Express

Background (1988)

Security Express Limited specializes in the cash-in-transit and cash-processing elements of the security service business. It has been operating since 1960 but was formerly a subsidiary of the De La Rue Group. Since the 2nd June 1985 the company has been operating as a United Kingdom subsidiary of the Australian Mayne Nickless Ltd company. Its take-over two years ago brings Security Express Limited into the largest security group in the world.

United Kingdom customers are served through a network of 24 branches. The core of the business is the collection and delivery of money. The company has a fleet of over 350 armoured vehicles and provides delivery services for such major customers as the Bank of England and the major clearing banks. Other customers include the Health Authorities and the large retail companies. A peripheral, but nonetheless important, part of the company's business covers such services as wage packet filling, credit checking, and the emptying of vending machines, telephone boxes, and auto-teller machines.

Employees

Sales turnover is around £25 million and as the company is part of the security service industry, all activities are regarded as labour intensive. Operations are continued on a 24 hour, seven day a week basis. 1,200 are 'core' employees and 1,500 are employed on a part time or seasonal basis. 60 per cent are male and 40 per cent female. The majority of women employees work on credit checking work at the company's cash centre. Around 500 of these are part timers, employed midweek only on Wednesdays and Thursdays.

Male employees work in teams manning armoured vehicles. Each crew has a minimum of two men and a maximum of four, depending on the value and volume of moneys in transit. A custodian is always present and is regarded as a supervisor. At least one driver/guard is always present. Some drivers have HGV licences. Because much of the maintenance work on vehicles is contracted out to a leasing company, Security Express employs only about a dozen fitters and maintenance engineers. Locks and alarms engineers are also employees of Security Express.

A closed shop is in operation for drivers and guards. The Transport and General Workers Union represents this group whilst ACTSS represents supervisory staff under a similar closed shop agreement. Since ASTMS were in effect voted out of the workplace by their residual members at Security Express (membership had fallen to 30 per cent of the potential group), salaried staff have no union representation.

The personnel function

Within the last two years the personnel management function has undergone considerable change. However, this re-organization of responsibilities is largely due to the change of policy *vis-à-vis* personnel management when Mayne Nickless took over from De La Rue. The Australian (Mayne Nickless) approach is for line management to have day to day responsibility for personnel management problems. These duties have been devolved down from the former specialist personnel section operating under De La Rue.

Under Mayne Nickless line managers also have access to the Security Express Director of Personnel for consultation on the detail of day to day personnel matters. Mayne Nickless policy is to employ one personnel manager in each of its subsidiary companies. In addition each region has an administrator with some personnel responsibility. This is primarily for salaried staff and senior managers. Matters concerning terms and conditions of employment for non salaried staff are dealt with by line management.

Introduction of technology

All aspects of developing technology that can be applied to improve the security of the armoured vans and the efficiency of the delivery service has been applied to the vehicles. Stronger metals improve the quality of the vehicle bodywork. High technology radio systems mean that there is more direct and regular control of the vehicles' movements. The quality of locks and security alarms has developed and these are now part of the features of the advanced armoured vehicle design. The techniques of potential raiders have developed in sophistication. Technological improvements built in to the vehicles help to improve the security of the cargo and the employee.

High technology developments included in customers' practices has had an effect on the work of Security Express employees. The major growth in auto-telling machines has meant business growth for the company. Wage packet filling represents a smaller proportion of overall business than would have been current five years ago. This is accounted for by the increase in the use of credit transfer arrangements. However, the provision of new services, such as via the bank and building society auto-teller machines, means that there is more actual money (as distinct from credit) in circulation.

Word processing systems have dramatically upgraded the clerical and secretarial function. a mainframe computer has dramatically improved accounting procedures.

Organizational Change

Four new branches have been 'spec' designed and opened and two others are 'on stream'. Advances in electronic sensing devices, locks and alarms meant that much of the new technology could not be introduced into the older branches. The design of the older buildings proved to be unsuitable because the new technology could not be operated effectively in the architecture of the 'old shapes'.

One organizational change which came about in the wake of the Mayne Nickless takeover concerned business strategy. Each branch is now run like an independent business and each branch manager has profit and budget responsibilities for what is effectively his business. New policy on personnel practice means that new business responsibility is combined with a new day to day personnel responsibility for non salaried staff. Although most managers accepted the new practices, some older managers were not so enthusiastic about taking on such a wide ranging role.

Employee reactions

Some technology was accepted by employees on the grounds that it enhanced their jobs, and in the context of the armoured vans, added something to improve their security. However, some employee resistance was encountered during Phase 1 of the introduction of high technology case equipment. One of the most vulnerable parts of a security operation comes at the point where staff are working between buildings and their own vehicle. The new case design was introduced to improve the security of cargo at this point. Employees were most concerned that the sophisticated technology built into the case would be accidentally triggered whilst the case was being carried in the vans.

Women were found to be more amenable than men to changes in their working practices, and to adapt more quickly. One of their main objections was that the new working conditions meant that there was no natural daylight to be seen from their office.

Employee Commitment

As the security industry is a labour intensive one and the company's 'only asset is its people', a good deal of emphasis is placed on regular and fairly informal consultation with employees. In return the workforce as a whole is considered to be extremely loyal and generally co-operative. One of the longer term results however is an ageing workforce in which staff turnover could be considered almost too low.

The workforce have usually been found to be in favour of what the company is planning. Consultation is a continuous process. All employees meet branch managers to discuss change, although each branch has at least one shop steward to represent them.

Trade Union Reactions

Security Express have adopted a flexibility agreement which came from their sister company, Parceline. Five years ago this agreement was current at the time that computerized parcel identification was being introduced. In effect this flexibility agreement is interpreted to mean 'any employee will undertake any required task'. No agreement on the 'single' issue of changing technology has been agreed.

Payment Systems

Staff are paid on the basis of a five day core working week. Extended hours worked to meet the greater volume of business are paid as incentive payments. These cover Saturday and Sunday and excess hours during the week. Methods of payment are thought of as very traditional and it is considered that it would not be possible to complete work on schedule if all staff were working on a consolidated salary basis.

Personnel Management

The demands of new technology and the requirements of the British Security Industrial Association together mean that certain training standards have to be fulfilled. The security industry has recently been de-regulated and for training purposes (in addition to other functions), the industry is now self-regulating. The Association ensures standards are being met by individual companies and Security Express Limited is subject to inspection three times a year. Recruitment and operating standards are also investigated. The company employs one trainer who has a central and co-ordinating role.

Due largely to the impact of the thrice yearly inspection, but also due to the additional skill demands of new technology, recruitment practices have been upgraded. Further education qualifications are now becoming a job requirement for supervisors. In the process of being introduced is a series of skill tests for road crew and cash centre staff. Until now no aptitude tests have been used at the recruitment stage. Personnel policy now favours their introduction at various planned stages over a 12 week probationary period. Additionally some cash centre operatives are required to work with more sophisticated money handling and counting machines and these require staff who are 'sympathetic to machines'. In the light of this finding the decision has been taken to bring in some objective testing techniques at staged points over a probationary period.

Scottish and Newcastle (Thistle Hotels)

Background (1988)

Thistle Hotels Ltd are a wholly owned subsidiary of Scottish and Newcastle Breweries. The chain of 34 hotels has eight based in London and aims at the 4 star sector of the hotel market. Hotels vary considerably in size and range between 10 and 830 bedrooms with an average bedroom capacity size of 130. Each hotel is run as a separate business. Total annual turnover is £100 million with a profit in the operating year 1986/87 of £14.7 million.

Employees total just over 4,000 with 2,344 full timers and 1,658 part timers. Employment levels are broadly proportional to numbers of bedrooms with a total of 4,000 rooms in all the hotels. Staff turnover is no higher than that for other companies in the hotel and catering sector but currently stands at 100 per cent per annum. The employee stability index is 55 per cent per annum.

Employees
Union density is 12 per cent and Thistle Hotels have a national agreement with the Hotel and Catering Workers Union (part of the GMWU). Two local agreements cover staff belonging to the TGWU at two hotels. Membership density may be higher or lower than 12 per cent in each hotel and this variable was thought to be related to the location of the hotel and the quality of the local shop steward.

The personnel function
Larger hotels employ personnel managers and sometimes training managers who report to the hotel managers. Relatively few personnel directives

are received from the central personnel team in London. Full responsibility
is devolved either to personnel managers in larger hotels or to whoever
carries responsibility for personnel matters in smaller hotels. In some cases
this role may be fulfilled by the financial controller.

The introduction of technology

A recent major capital investment programme of £100 million has upgraded fixtures and fittings. It has also upgraded the booking and billing
procedures at the hotel front desks by computerizing what were previously
manual tasks completed on typewriters.

The parent company, Scottish and Newcastle Breweries, have used
a mainframe for management accounting, bought ledger work and for the
company payroll for many years. Payroll details for Thistle Hotels are
supplied on a manual system and linked into the parent company mainframe. There have been no changes to these procedures but IBM Personal
Computers have just been introduced into each of the hotels. The main
reason is for budgetry uses but later applications are likely to be for
management accounting.

Details of the training needs of managers and supervisors which
were formerly inputted into a word processor have now been transferred
into a computer data base. Career Development Review Forms are
completed by managers each year, the information analyzed and then used
to place people on lists to denote their preferences, availability and
transferability *vis-à-vis* other posts within the company. This principle of
capturing career profiles and ambitions has recently been extended to
include waiters and chefs.

Organizational Change

The computerization of the front office booking and billing procedures has
had the most effect on work patterns. Computerization has reached
varying degrees of sophistication. In some hotels the front office operations are linked to the other points of sale in the hotel, for example the bar
and restaurant.

The major advantages of computerization were seen to be speedier
operations, 'cleaner' and more understandable bills, and the need to
produce one copy of the final bill only. Bills are only printed out when the

customer asks for them and this is usually at the time of departure. Previous procedures involved using typewriters and adding additional items during the course of the customer's stay.

Thistle Hotels plans to computerize all its hotels in due course. However, the exercise is seen to be one in which the level of service to the customer can be immediately improved, but also one in which there are no immediate advantages in terms of cost reduction or changes in staffing levels.

One of the major difficulties with the booking and billing computers has been the fact that technology is developing so fast that an existing system can soon appear to be out of date. The replacement of systems can present the problem of staff adaptation and the feeling that the hotels are 'guinea pigs' for the hardware and software.

Nonetheless, there are also particular advantages for the marketing department. Information that would have previously been recorded separately on, for example, a customer's nationality, type of company, length of stay, and total bill, can now be automatically accessed. This removes the clerical tasks associated with recording this information from the jobs of the front office receptionists.

Due to this expansion of front office computerization, the small centrally based team of three systems planners has now expanded to five. They advise management on up to date systems and new installations, write programmes and undertake budgetry modelling.

Employee reactions
Staff employed on front desk operations have taken a very positive view of changed procedures, regarding the computers as positive aids to their jobs. Much routine paper work has been removed such that a computerized hotel no longer has any need for a typewriter at all. An additional feature for employees is the improvement in their perception of their marketability. A skilled receptionist has experience in fax, telex and switchboard, together with the new booking and billing procedures, and as such can enter an increasingly buoyant labour market in which employers are competing for skilled staff.

Employee Commitment

Personnel staff have a particular role in discussing communications strategies with managers. A wide range of techniques are used including team briefing (a method implemented with the aid of the Industrial Society), informal lunch gatherings and ceremonies for long service or other awards. Consultative meetings are held every month in some hotels.

Although the advent of the booking and billing systems did not entail any change to existing communication methods, employees were informed well in advance of the changes that they could expect. In addition, those with personnel responsibility do undertake random type tests to check that the appropriate information is being disseminated to hotel staff!

Trade Union Reactions

Annual negotiations are conducted to set minimum pay rates for the company over and above those set by the Wages Council for the industry. In addition, information is provided to the union representatives at an annual 'Disclosure Meeting' on such matters for example as new craft apprenticeship schemes and other training initiatives. No matter relating to technical change as an issue separate from other issues has been raised at either of these forums by the union. No new technology or flexibility agreements have been negotiated.

Some local level negotiations may be found to be necessary in hotels in which there is an above average union presence either in numerical terms or where the shop steward is particularly active. However changes at hotel level usually have less to do with technical innovation than service innovation. For example, proposals to introduce drinks trays into rooms would mean additional tasks for existing staff and could become a negotiating issue. As manning levels are the responsibility of the hotel manager, negotiations of this kind would fall under his or her jurisdiction.

Displaced Workers

Technology, even in the office booking and billing context in which most working practice changes are experienced, has never been regarded as a manning issue either by hotel management or by employees. Even in the larger hotels it is not expected that computerization will have implications for manning levels. Hotel managers tend to regard computerization as an opportunity to improve customer service rather than an opportunity to reduce the number of receptionists.

Payment Systems

Hotel managers have the discretion to pay their staff above the nationally agreed minimum rates within reasonable limits. A productivity bonus is in operation for front desk staff. Criteria are occupancy or average room rate with seasonal adjustments and six monthly reviews. Improvements in the speed and efficiency of the booking and billing procedures are technical changes which can have beneficial effects on the quality of service provision. This development can in turn have implications for occupancy levels and for employee benefits in terms of pay through the productivity bonus scheme.

A bonus scheme is also in operation for all management teams including head office managers. Thistle Hotels also operate an employee profit share scheme for staff with two years service who have been employed for 25 hours or more a week and who are currently employed when the company has had a good financial year.

Personnel Management

In response to technical and other change, personnel has had a particular role in promoting a high level of awareness of the need for training. Apart from the overall business objective of improving services to the customer, personnel promotes training as a method for improving people, for facilitating change and for improving communications. Personnel also has responsibility for promoting the employee relations philosophy through line management that the wide ranging communications strategy is based on an open and frank style. Although training and communications may be devolved either to the departmental head or the hotel manager, responsibility for training and communication exists actively at every level in the organization down to department level.

The extension of the use of the Career Development Review Forms to include waiters and chefs was facilitated by the transfer of the career data base to a computer data base. It was intended to increase recognition of this group and to improve individual's motivation to stay with the company.

Some adjustments have also been made to terms and conditions of employment to improve employee's career progression. Definitions of management are being extended to include supervisors in the lower tiers of management. As Thistle Hotels employ staff on one of only two types of employment contract, this move benefits supervisors who thereby become entitled to join the company pension scheme after two years rather than four. This continues a policy of 'flattening' out the company structure which has been developing over the last three or four years.

Personality profiling programmes have been introduced on VDUs and are used selectively but particularly in the recruitment process for the annual intake of graduates. The parent company's occupational health department undertakes regular tests for people working with VDUs. A paper on the health risks associated with VDUs has been circulated to managers.

Technical change has not led to organizational change such that involvement for personnel managers has been required to be of a high profile nature. The manpower considerations arising from technical change have not been particularly complex and employee response has been experienced as positive. However, there has been some concern that employees should develop confidence on the computer in order to avoid becoming 'computer conscious' to the exclusion of the customer!

Thomas Cook

Background (May 1989)

The Thomas Cook Group Limited, a wholly owned subsidiary of Midland Group, is the largest travel organization in the world with outlets in 146 countries throughout the world.

This international network provides a wide range of travel and travel-related financial services operating under similar management controls – not just a spread of associated or franchised travel agencies and *bureaux de change*.

On a geographical basis, Thomas Cook operates in the United Kingdom, Europe, Canada, the Middle East, the Far East, India, Australia, New Zealand, the South Pacific and in the USA.

In the relatively few business areas of the world where there are no Thomas Cook branches, an authorized representative is appointed and will generally offer a similar range of services.

Thomas Cook, whose international headquarters are based in Peterborough, has three main product areas:

Leisure Travel
The retail network, which has the largest market share in the UK, comprises over 350 sales outlets which specialise in all forms of travel. The shops, all fully automated, offer all major tour operators' holidays, its own 'Faraway' brand range, and specializes in personal customer service.

Business Travel Management
The company provides a wide range of travel services to multinational, national and regional corporations and currently manages the travel of over 12,000 client companies worldwide. It is the largest business travel agency in the world.

Travellers Cheques and Foreign Currency

Thomas Cook, which currently has approximately 16 per cent of
the worldwide travellers cheque market, operates in association
with European Travellers Cheques International and is a member
of the MasterCard travellers cheque scheme. Other financial
services include the purchase and sale of foreign currency notes
through bulk note dealing operations in London, Paris and Hong
Kong. Some 165 currencies both in notes and coins are handled
by these centres who supply Thomas Cook retail branches, other
travel agents, building societies and banks worldwide.

Employees

The numerical total and distribution of Thomas Cook employees is a
complex picture, primarily due to the placement of about eight and a half
thousand employees throughout the world. Around 6,500 are UK based
with the majority employed in the company's retail shops. The remaining
employees provide a wide range of support services with a larger number
undertaking automated administrative work. Qualified accounting staff
have a particularly important role to play, because in a low margin business
the company's priority must be to retain control of costs. Consequently,
the company is very financially orientated. The worldwide administrative
centre and headquarters is based at Peterborough, employing around 1,400
people including the key accounting and other support functions, e.g.
systems, marketing, personnel.

The former worldwide headquarters at Berkeley Street in London's
West End, is now Thomas Cook's largest travel shop employing around
200 staff. Also located in Berkeley Street is the Thomas Cook Wholesale
Foreign Money Dealing operation providing foreign currency for the
travel shops, building societies and banks.

Trade union representation in the UK is provided by the TSSA
which has sole bargaining rights at Thomas Cook. Membership levels are
at around 20 per cent in the UK.

Human resources

The director of the Human Resources Department is a member of the
Senior Management Group – the premier operational and decision making
body. The Group Board meets less frequently and is concerned primarily
with the Company's long term strategy.

A revised personnel structure was established in June 1988. There
are four major human resources departments providing full personnel and

training services to the major sectors of the company; these are the Consumer, Corporate, Finance and Operations and Central Services Sectors.

These operational Human Resource departments are supported by a small Group Human Resource function which provides the policy development and advice and guidance service for all the Human Resource activities within the Group worldwide. This Group function comprises specialists in Reward and Benefits, Employee Relations and Training, Development and Succession Planning.

Within the Consumer Sector there is a regionalized personnel force which has responsibility for 31 regions. Most personnel officers have responsibility for three to five regions and maintain a strong functional relationship with their respective regional managers.

The introduction of technology

Thomas Cook operates in the vanguard of technological development, particularly in the area of data transfer. Over the last eight to nine years data transfer techniques have been integrated in a significant way at retail shop level. This reflects the introduction by tour operators of huge on-line computer reservation systems. Thus, their own systems and those of the major tour operators and airlines enable Thomas Cook sales staff to check details of the availability of most holidays and seat availability for nearly every flight. The information becomes available within a matter of seconds.

Organizational Change

Large Research and Development sections at Peterborough are fully engaged in the continuous updating of automation systems, particularly in the field of telecommunications. Development is focused on data and voice transfer techniques and on telecommunications networking. As one travel operation amongst many, Thomas Cook is selling the same type of holiday or business travel product and service as its competitors. Thus, the achievement of a competitive advantage in terms of the provision of customer service is seen to be of vital importance. The effective employment of telecommunications technology is regarded as a key area through which the quality and speed of customer service can be continually updated and improved.

One of the net effects of developing from the previous range of manual techniques to working from computer terminals is the saving in information search time in which branch staff are engaged. Consequently, more productive time is released for activities such as product selling and the provision of high quality customer service.

The leisure retail branches currently provide the widest range of leisure travel products and foreign exchange. However, until four or five years ago the majority of these branches also provided business travel services. However, business travel services have progressively come to be regarded as a separate activity from the leisure trade, and a network of around 70 business travel centres are now established around the country. Integral to the structure of the business travel centre is the provision of a dedicated administrative support group manned by clerical staff. This structure further supports the operational principle that skilled sales employees should be released from time spent on administrative work or information search work for effective product selling and high quality customer interaction.

The same principle has been applied to the employment structure of the leisure outlets. Branch-based clerical assistants are increasingly carrying the bulk of the administrative workload, allowing travel consultants and senior travel consultants to concentrate on customer contact. This organizational change aimed at improvements in customer service could not be said to be directly driven by technical change. However, the level of technical development was such that its effective utilization facilitated organizational changes which resulted in clear cut benefits for the quality of customer service.

With the growth of more airlines and airline services, more services and choices become available for the discerning customer. The two-pronged strategy of improved 'over the counter' service, separated to some extent from, but supported by, fully automated administrative backup is the pattern for current and future progress.

Automation of a related kind was also a factor in the establishment of the separate business travel centres. The comprehensiveness and complexity of new systems, notably the Travicom and DPAS systems was such that new areas of specialization tended to develop to shape employees' working time. Therefore, considerable advantages could be seen in structuring employment so that Business Travel Consultants could act effectively in providing a full Corporate Sales service whilst automation staff provided administrative backup.

In the larger business travel centres (between a third and a half of centres) the managerial structure has been revised. The former assistant

Branch Manager is now the Operations Manager and a new position of Manager, Quality Control has been established to supervise the dedicated administration support sections. Non-automated administration in leisure branches is now carried out by another newly established role of Branch Assistant.

Both leisure and business travel operations now have access to increased support from the Peterborough headquarters. A Help Desk can tackle branch difficulties in adapting to the technical demands of new systems.

Employee reactions

A natural reluctance to change was thought to be one of the factors which Thomas Cook faced in the context of technical change. However, some initial anxiety of the unknown often gave way to later enthusiasm. In other contexts the learning curve was still being worked through some time after the introduction of technical change.

Older and more mature staff have had to rethink the ways in which vast quantities of information is handled. Slightly older supervisors in particular (aged between 30 and 40) were amongst those who were conscious of their own need for retraining. The younger generation of employees were found to have no overall difficulties in adapting, although the Company was prepared to recognize and resolve some individual anxieties.

Employee Commitment and Trade Union Involvement

The company has placed a good deal of emphasis on regular communication. A quarterly staff council on which the trade union sits is supplemented by regular staff meetings at branch and regional level.

The level and frequency of employee and union consultation tends to be in proportion to the degree of change anticipated or experienced. If an issue arose in which extensive change featured, then full consultation activities would follow. In the event, however, no situation relating to technical change has arisen which to date generated any significant conflict between management and trade union. Similarly, during the course of annual pay negotiations the increasing degree of automation has not featured as a negotiating issue.

Hitherto, automation has occurred in a progressive fashion and the company has yet to face the implications of dramatic change in this sector.

Where automation or any other matter requiring major change is planned, procedures for setting up a Joint Working Party with management, employee and union representatives would occur. For example, a Joint Working Party was set up to deal with job evaluation, performance appraisal, Saturday working arrangements and one is currently considering the possible benefits of 'annual hours'.

Displaced Workers

Technical change did not result in immediate staff reductions, although the employment implications of technical change are veiled to some extent by the coinciding development of the overall business.

At the Peterborough headquarters the accounting work for the leisure and business branches is a centralized activity. Large numbers of cash books, receipts and counterfoils are received daily from the branches. These require handling and coding on a daily basis. Until eight or nine years ago this was predominantly a manual task which later became a data entry task for the accounting department. These tasks are currently completed by VDU operators and eventually this function is expected to become an on-line function with the responsibility for input being relocated to the branches. The precise employment implications of this change have yet to be determined.

Very few employees have been faced with enforced redundancy from the company with most instances being due to a combination of business reasons, with technical change not necessarily the dominant factor. However, some redeployment of accounts clerks who formerly handled daily information from the branches has been necessary due to automated accounting systems becoming even more sophisticated and effective.

The effective management of displaced workers has involved a strong personnel input. A number of personnel officers were sent to redeployment training courses and a walk-in staff counselling centre can be set up as necessary to manage any major redeployment situation.

Branch managers have responsibility for on-the-job training and re-training. They also provide significant input into distance learning courses which are extensively used by Thomas Cook. The Training Department at Peterborough has 10 full time staff engaged in operator training, sales techniques training, airfare construction and foreign exchange courses. These are just part of a comprehensive range of training modules regularly provided to support headquarters and branch staff.

Payment Systems

When the level of automation has increased there has been considerable debate about job design. However, despite a well developed points based job evaluation system, jobs which incorporated new contact with data processing techniques, or which were in themselves new, were not necessarily revised upwards under the weighting systems. Heightened 'dexterity' for example was a factor, but this did not necessarily bring with it the factor of heightened 'knowledge'. However, the Company is now introducing a fully integrated reward, performance and development approach under the generic heading of 'Gemini'. One key factor to the scheme is the operation of total performance related pay from January 1990. Central to these new processes is 'Role Evaluation' which replaces the current traditional job evaluation systems and derives its base from assessing the knowledge, skills and aptitudes an individual needs to effectively carry out their job.

Role Evaluation covers every single employee at all levels in the UK organization. The process specifically identifies the Information Technology knowledge and skills required in each role as a discrete area of evaluation.

Within some of the major data entry departments, 'key depression rates' (monitoring the speed of operation) are included as a factor in an incentive payments scheme which has implications for salary progression.

Personnel Management

Personnel involvement with technical change has been at the highest level of strategic debate allowing identification of its implications and the development of the human resource strategy to minimize any adverse impact on staff. Within the 'middle ground' the main interchange was between line managers and the telecommunications and systems developers. However, personnel activity is generally described as 'proactive' and any implications of technical change for the Company's employees are handled within this framework.

A Health and Safety Officer has responsibility for constant monitoring of the health and safety implications of technology. Information is made available to data entry operators in particular in order to dispel any unrealistic anxieties. Information distilled from the Health and Safety Executive's work on, for example, ergonomic factors are reported to managers in order to ensure that such factors are taken into account in the daily working environment. A forum of managers of major VDU usage departments has been established where the implications of automation are discussed.

TSB Group

Background (1988)

Following recent re-organization, public flotation and acquisition of new companies, the TSB Group plc currently operates with the following company structure:

The TSB Group comprises four banks established according to broad geographical region. In descending order of size these are TSB England and Wales, TSB Scotland, TSB Northern Ireland and TSB Channel Islands. Formerly savings banks under the previous and more devolved structure of 16 autonomous regional banks, these four now provide a full range of banking services. Until 1976 the banks did not make loans and had no business customers. They specialized in providing a personal service to individual savings customers. The fully fledged development of the four banks into banks providing facilities, including corporate lending in 1987, has brought the TSB into a very competitive banking and financial services marketplace.

The TSB Trust Company provides unit trusts and insurance services. TSB Trustcard issues credit cards. TSB Commercial Holdings consists of three main operations. United Dominions Trust is a finance house, itself divided into four operations: point of sale lending, direct consumer lending, corporate lending and debt financing. The UDT Bank operates banking and finance house activities in the Irish Republic. Swan National operates car and van rental, car leasing services and a chain of garages throughout the United Kingdom. The Target Group and the Hill Samuels Group are very recent acquisitions of the TSB Group. Total annual income for the group for the year ending November 1986 was £827 million.

Employees
The total number of staff employed in the TSB Group as a whole

(excluding Target and Hill Samuel) is just over 30,500. This figure includes part-timers who are included as half of a full time equivalent employee. 22,500 (74 per cent) are employed in banking whilst 2,100 are employed by the TSB Trust Company. 350 are employed at the TSB Group headquarters, 1,000 by the TSB Trustcard, and the remainder within the member companies of TSB Commercial Holdings.

The majority of the TSB Trust Company staff are based at Andover, although the salesforce operates throughout the country. Trustcard employees are employed at either the computer centre in Crawley or at one of several offices in Brighton. United Dominions Trust's finance and sales staff are employed through a branch network with a Headquarters at New Barnet. A small corporate loans division is located in the City of London. Consumer finance for direct lending to members of the public is centralized at one location and UDT as a whole has a centralized management unit. Swan National staff are split between London and Leicester. Swan National Leasing is based in Croydon. Swan National Rentals is based in Uxbridge and Leicester, although there is a network of branches around the country. Swan National Motors has a number of garages which are at diverse locations around the country operating under their own trading names.

Trade union membership is at a high density within the banks at around 80 per cent of staff. A union membership agreement is in existence, although under the current law this amounts to a statement of intent due to the fact that it has not been balloted. In England and Wales, Scotland and Northern Ireland the union with negotiating rights is the Banking Insurance and Finance Union. In Northern Ireland the Irish Bank Officers Association is recognized. Staff within United Dominions Trust and TSB Trust Company are represented by BIFU although separate agreements are negotiated in each case. Northern Ireland employees of United Dominions Trust are represented by APEX. In the United Dominions Trust Bank an ASTMS agreement was negotiated although this has fallen into disuse more recently. Sales staff employed by the TSB Trust Company are not unionized. Sales staff employed by United Dominions Trust are covered by the main agreement settled with BIFU.

Until 1987 a centralized bargaining structure was used for bank staff. Negotiations were carried out with BIFU at the group Head Office in London. Currently policy is for the devolution of bargaining structure to the four individual banks. Data processing staff previously negotiated separately but also centrally. This covered data processing staff in the banks, TSB Trustcard, TSB Trust Company and Head Office. Data processing staff employed by United Dominions Trust were included in settlements agreed for **all** staff working for UDT. Similarly all Trust Company staff except the data processors negotiated separately. Following the pattern now agreed for BIFU banking staff there is a process of devolving negotiations down to company level.

The personnel function

The main unit companies of the group have a devolved responsibility for operating their particular businesses. Each company has its own personnel department, whilst the Group also has a personnel department at the Group Head Office in London. The purpose of this department is to develop policy and strategy, and in addition, to assist companies with the practice and implementation of personnel policies. The department is headed by a Director of Personnel who reports to the Group Managing Director.

Bank branches in England and Wales are divided into regions which are further divided into districts. In Scotland there are two regions only and in Northern Ireland and the Channel Islands branches report directly to Head Office. Personnel staff are employed at regional level, together with Field Personnel Managers and Field Training Managers in each region. The Field Personnel Manager has responsibility for recruitment.

Introduction of technology

Technological innovation and implementation has had, and continues to have, a significant impact on the component companies of the TSB Group. However, technical change was first absorbed some years ago in a number of contexts. Trustcard was fairly highly automated from the start when it was set up in the early 1980s. The level of technology used in 1987 is on a par with that first implemented in the early 1980s and there have been no significant further changes. The TSB Trust Company has a large computer capability, although throughout its history the company has always had a certain level of technology. Development within United Dominions Trust has progressed periodically. In the 1970s a computerized collections system was introduced and at the time this represented a high level of technical sophistication. The system has recently been radically revised. More recently computer links mean improved communications with branches.

Prior to the reorganization of the 16 TSB Banks into the current four, the banks as a whole were organized into consortia for computer purposes. One of these covered the whole of England and Wales, apart from the South East of England, and another covered Scotland. Historically the

TSB did not have such a strong branch presence in the South East. In the 1970s an advanced counter system (on-line real time) was introduced into the branch network in England and Wales, although excluding the South East. Scotland had developed its own on-line real time system and this was not compatible with that used in England and Wales until recently, when strategic decisions were taken to bring the Scottish system in line with the England/Wales system and to extend the main on-line system into the South East.

The counter system has all transactions organised on an account basis. A terminal placed on the counter provides access to detailed information about each account. A counter clerk can key in changes and access all relevant information, whether the customer has a cheque or deposit account. Two computer centres cover the country's branches and details of personal loans are handled by the same computer.

In the future it is conceivable that counter operations as such will not exist and the TSB is experimenting with counterless branches. The branch network is extremely expensive and 'robot' branches of a kind are under consideration although only one currently exists. In addition some branches have been designated as 'key branches' specializing in corporate business whilst others will continue to specialize in the personal customer business.

In the branch back offices automation will have an impact on a number of activities. Included is a sophisticated form of word processing. A letter centrally originated can be sent to different branches. Global marketing techniques will give way to a special form of targeting of individual account holders. Links into customer files mean that literature can be targeted to individuals on the basis of information provided by the computer link.

CHAPS is the system used by the major clearing houses, including the TSB, for the automatic moving of money between different banks. All moneys are cleared through a central computer in the City of London. Currently cheques are physically transported between the banks by security companies. In the future the development of 'truncation' would mean that cheques would not need to be transported. The sorting of cheques is a procedure which is currently automated but which requires staff time.

Whilst procedures have been rationalized, affecting staff working methods, some other procedures are entirely new and are the result of technology providing services for the general public. TSB is collaborating in a working party on electronic funds transfer point of sale systems. Customers can pay retailers with cards which are not credit cards. The customer's account is automatically debited and the retailer's account is automatically credited with the correct amount. Speedlink is a system for customers to effect transactions on their accounts by telephone. Customers can use their telephones to order the payment of bills, for example.

Autoteller machines housed inside or often outside branches are taking on an increasing range of cash withdrawals, cash deposit, and balance enquiry type transactions. These remove the business of 'routine' bank business form the sphere of the counter clerk.

Organizational Change

Much organizational change can be attributed directly to business strategy. The marketplace for banks has become more competitive and more innovative. Technology has a place as one of the tools for effecting rationalization of existing services and the provision of entirely new services in an increasingly competitive market. In this context it is by no means a straightforward matter to identify organizational change which is a direct result of changing technology. It would be most accurate to say that to some extent 'market pressures' and 'technology' go together. However in the TSB context organizational change of the most far reaching nature has come about as a result of 'market forces'; technology becomes the means by which adaptation to the market can be effected.

As a preliminary strategy to public flotation the re-organization of the 16 banks into four regionally based banks was completed in 1983. The flotation completed in September 1986 did alter the organization, although the company entities did not change. Reorganization tended to affect more senior staff at managerial level, rather than those at branch level. Those employed at branch level around the country found on the whole that their jobs were changing and expanding at the same time. As some former skills were incorporated into the activities of the computers, so no actual vacuum appeared. The expanding range of services and the expanding volume of work meant that their jobs were not deskilled, but rather the reverse.

Technology has had a significant impact on the role of branch staff. Not only does the counter technology provide accounting functions, it also provides instant access to account information. Business strategy requires a new responsiveness to customer needs and the tailoring of products to the individual customer. With the aid of the counter technology the counter staff can access the information without themselves needing to have acquired in-depth financial information. The role of the staff is developing in the sense that currently and in the future, they will be becoming highly skilled at dealing with customers; confident and efficient (with the aid of the computer) information providers. In the future, staff are likely to have more customer contact and to become 'sellers' of services to those customers.

The increasing need for staff to provide advisory services to customers, at the same time that simple processing operations are automated, means that fewer staff will be required at the lower clerical levels but more will be needed at a slightly higher level. It is the latter group who are required to have the right temperament in order to act as skilled 'information providers'. It is also expected that the introduction of expert systems will have a qualitative impact on employment. Their introduction into branches can aid such staff in the provision of high quality advice to customers.

The automation of counter work has meant that the more complex tasks that staff are required to handle have been relocated from the counter operation back to the office operation. However, developments are now taking place in back office operations which will have considerable impact on the work of staff. Changes in both contexts mean that the fairly time consuming 'chore' activities, such as writing down figures and generally handling them correctly, have been removed from the workload of the staff to the activity of the computer.

Such role changes currently, and in the future, have considerable impact on the training and recruitment activities of personnel management. Traditional recruitment policy in the TSB was to recruit school leavers at the age of sixteen, to provide them with all round training and job security; a 'job for life' for many if not all. Technology implies a change in the 'sort' of person recruited. New employee specifications evolve from new responsibilities.

Employee reactions
As developments in accounting and information systems were taking place, so the bank was extending its range of services. As these two trends broadly coincided, employees tended to regard the technology as an aid to coping with changes. Employees were thought to accept change because in most contexts change was more or less incremental and a development of a set of technological changes that had been going on for some time. However, when the main on-line computer system was introduced into the South East region within the last two years, 'teething problems', largely due to technical problems, were experienced. No gap in training provision was identified, but staff had to become acclimatized to working practices

which were significantly different from those previously established. In addition some older customers were felt to have some resistance to the use of automatic teller machines.

Employee Commitment

Reorganization of the bank into four main banks was the spur to the establishment of consultative procedures which were not in existence previously. In 1982 a 'Consultative Communications Procedure' agreement was introduced to cover banking staff. However, although technological change was included in the items to be covered by the procedures, it was one amongst other items including product development and operational change. It covered the stages of change as follows: concept, planning and implementation. Regular consultative meetings began to take place at the highest level; participants included the Group Managing Director and General Secretary of BIFU.

Trade Union Reactions

United Dominions Trust staff were covered by an agreement which set up consultation procedures similar to those for bank staff. In this instance, however, the agreement was called a 'Technology Agreement', although in the event it covered all forms of organizational change.

Clauses relating to technology for banking staff in their own agreement covered such eventualities as deskilling; staff will not suffer any discrimination in terms and conditions of employment. Also, if new jobs are created preferential treatment will be given to existing staff. Under job security clauses employees will be offered alternative employment.

Displaced Workers

No employees were made redundant as a direct result of technology. However, a few were made redundant as a result of re-organization prior to flotation. Much of the impact of re-organization was felt by senior staff, and some senior managers were made redundant when the 16 banks became four.

Payment Systems

TSB have undertaken no restructuring of payment systems as a direct result of employees' increased contact with technology. Technology was felt to be part of the jobs and not the whole of them. In addition, due to the fact that jobs were expanding into new areas whilst the old areas were being absorbed by the computer, jobs could not be described as deskilled or significantly re-skilled such that pay would need to be re-assessed. Established relativities have not been disturbed by technology and technology has not been an issue in pay bargaining.

Personnel Management

Historically speaking the personnel management function has not been closely integrated with the formulation of business strategy. Personnel professionals have been involved with training provision and with union and employee communications. However, because of a higher level involvement with planning activities the personnel function is now being drawn in towards strategic decision making.

There is a corporate planning department at Group Head Office. Development plans are fed into this section at Group Headquarters from the separate banks and TSB Group companies. These plans are reviewed by a team of people including systems, planning, technology, finance and personnel specialists. Plans are then discussed with each company or bank. Briefings are prepared for the Group Managing Director. The review team are currently particularly conscious of reaching a balance between the devolving of responsibility to individual companies and getting value from the size of the Group.

At branch level the personnel function is responsible for the control of the branch establishment system. This calculates, on a work measurement basis agreed with the union, the number of staff required in the branch. The system can be used by the personnel function as a forecasting tool. The estimated improvements or changes can be keyed in and the appropriate staffing level will be calculated by the system. Systems and planning staff are also involved in the staffing implications of changes. However, the personnel function controls the system (technical and human) which calculates the staffing levels from the information input.

The TSB has consistently had a policy of recruiting school leavers and then 'training them to do everything'. However, the advent of technology in the branches has brought about a change in emphasis. 15 years ago a new recruit would have been 'hidden away' at the back of the branch until he or she had the skills and confidence to progress to the more demanding counter roles. Such is the impact of technology on the skills required of the counter staff operating terminals that the more technically demanding work has now moved from the counter staff to the back office staff. Consequently, although all staff are still trained in all processes, the pattern on their 'career' progression through the branches' separate activities has subtly altered. Younger staff work on the counter sooner! The impact on the personnel contribution is that there is a new training need to equip staff with the confidence, presence and skill to become information providers at an earlier age and for a demanding group of customers of all ages and requirements!

Overall the major area of activity linking technology and personnel is training. Personnel staff at regional level are heavily involved in the provision of training. At branch level this is organized on the whole as 'on the job training'. This can either be described as 'on the machine training' (in which staff are removed from their jobs and are trained on the machines which will assist them in carrying out their jobs), or as 'self-teaching'. This latter provides a teaching package through which the learner works until he or she has mastered the skills in his or her own way.

There has been a fairly strong growth in the number of part time employees. The proportion of part timers is now just over one for every three junior clerical staff employed. However, part timers are a relatively small proportion of union members and of clerical staff as a whole. Part timers recruited tend to be former employees. Many of them, but not all, are women who are returning to work following family responsibilities. This has a particular training advantage for TSB. Training responsibilities are already a major aspect of personnel work at the TSB. As part time workers are recruited to cover growth peaks in business (at lunchtime, on Mondays, at branches in marketplaces and at some seasonal points) it is of particular advantage if they can be quickly re-integrated into branch practices without further extensive exposure to training.

Woolwich Equitable Building Society

Background (May 1989)

Woolwich Equitable Building Society is currently the fourth largest building society in Britain with assets of £13.5 billion. There is a large gap in asset size between the first three building societies (led by the Halifax with £40.5 billion) and the Woolwich.

On the 1st January 1987 the Building Societies Act 1986 came into effect. This allows a development of 90 per cent of the Woolwich Building Society's business to be in mortgage and investment, with up to 10 per cent of total business in other financial services. Now available are short term unsecured consumer loans and longer term consumer loans which take house ownership as security. A wider range of home insurance is also available, as is a network of over 400 'Cashbase' autoteller machines which can be used for cash withdrawal, bill and standing order payments.

A subsidiary company, Woolwich Homes (1987) Limited, was set up to provide low cost housing and to extend home ownership to be within the reach of more individuals. Twelve schemes have been built so far providing over 1,000 low cost or sheltered homes. Through another subsidiary, Woolwich Property Services Limited, the Society is developing an estate agency network mainly based in the South East. Others have been created individually or jointly with insurance companies to handle various financial services.

Recent developments, including Acts of Parliament, which continue to deregulate the financial services markets as a whole, have meant that the Woolwich continues to lend in a very competitive mortgage market. In addition, the recent redevelopment of other financial services brings the Woolwich into markets in which it faces increasing competition from other building societies and financial institutions.

Employees
Staff employed number almost 5,500 including 730 part timers. Two thirds

of the staff are employed within 16 regions in the growing network of 550 branches. These branches cover the whole of England, Wales, Scotland and Northern Ireland although there is a heavy concentration in the South East of England. The remaining one third are employed in three Headquarters sites. 300 work at the head office in Woolwich, 1,000 work at the main corporate and administrative centre at Bexleyheath and a further 300 at Worthing. 100 staff work in a satellite location concerned with supply and printing offices and a further 230 are currently employed or on secondment to Woolwich Homes (1987) Limited and other subsidiary companies.

An independent staff association (Woolwich Independent Staff Association) has been representing the majority of staff over the last 40 years. The association was certified as independent in 1977. It has negotiating rights and consultation structures for all staff up to C grade. This effectively includes all staff and lower graded managers. Any issue affecting terms and conditions can become a matter for discussion and negotiation. A network of regional and local representatives cover several branches and departments each and can assist staff with their grievances with line management if requested or consult on matters of mutual interest.

The personnel function

Working under the General Manager (Personnel and Training) are personnel professionals, including a Training and Development Manager, and Regional and Senior Personnel Officers. Three/four personnel officers work under the Senior Personnel Officer (head office) and six personnel officers work for the Senior Regional Personnel Officer. Following the merger with the Gateway, personnel officers have been placed regionally which allows more emphasis on local contact within branches in the regions.

The Training Departments has been organized on a regional basis with localized training officers, as well as other training officers covering head office departments. The residential training college, Foxbury, in Chislehurst, Kent, is heavily used, especially for the more senior management courses. Over 42 staff are involved in continuing the development of departmental growth from its beginnings nearly thirty years ago.

Introduction of technology

The whole field of transactions undertaken at Woolwich can be described as 'Data Processing driven'. 350 staff are employed in data-processing development work. The Woolwich was the first building society to install on-line terminals onto the branch counters as distinct from back office systems in 1979. The IBM mainframe is supplemented by personal computers and by viewdatas.

Information can be instantly accessible from centralized databases. Updates on mortgages and quotations on insurance policies, according to mortgage specification, are available at the point of sale. The legal requirement to provide information which is accurate can place demands on the database and on the counter staff to interpret accurately.

Future developments include the requirement to streamline computer systems to improve database. This forms part of the plan to prepare for future decentralization from the head office – decision making being developed further to the branch level operations, as well as the probable extension of electronic mail transmission.

Organizational Change

Technology has eased the monitoring processes for branch operations and individual staff progress. Each person at branch level has a numbered code. Managers can gain information through the computer against this code. This can have implications for the allocation of work within the branch and for the assessment of training needs. Information can be available on the speed and quality of transactions which the counter clerk, for example, undertakes. Those who do not progress satisfactorily in their handling of new computer technology and new products can either be referred for further training or temporarily relocated to the back office tasks in the branch. Job descriptions are flexible enough to allow for such changes. 'Cashier/typists' work is primarily on the counters and 'typist/ cashiers' work has an emphasis on duties other than counter work, although counter work will be included.

One of the key organizational aspects of the growth in information technology was the recognition that the Society was becoming increasingly dependent on its mainframe computer. Many systems including the payroll now run on the mainframe with back up facilities being increasingly provided by personal computers.

Additionally, as a 'technology driven' organization the Woolwich is necessarily dependent on the systems designs of the data processing team. However, one of the major difficulties experienced at organizational level was due to the fact that data processors did not always have the initial knowledge of management systems and senior managers' methods of working in order to introduce the effective integration of management and

data processing systems. Data processors tended not to have line management experience, and some managers tended to use some of the data
processing systems only when they felt that they had to. Current pilot
electronic mail studies have been viewed with some doubt but the project
is in hand for full implementation throughout the Societies.

Employee reactions

The majority of Woolwich employees accept that technology removes
many routine clerical tasks from their jobs. Those in managerial and
supervisory positions find that technology helps to improve the quality of
information on which they can take decisions. There has also been a
tendency towards the centralization of activities which were once undertaken manually at branch level and vice versa. First and second stage letters
sent out from branches in the event of mortgage arrears were formerly
produced by hand at each branch. Information is now centrally computerized and initial arrears letters are produced automatically. In such ways
as this the clerical workload of branch staff has eased, whilst at the same
time the range of financial services provided at branch level has increased.

Most branch staff have been able to adapt to their changing roles.
However, there was thought to be a difference in ability to adapt as and
between younger and slightly older employees. Younger staff had often
had some exposure to computers before taking up their jobs with the
Woolwich. But those who are currently in the late 30s age group and
upwards were felt to have a slightly higher than average turnover rate in
their jobs. The stated reason for leaving was thought to be different from
the actual reasons for leaving. Older staff were not brought up with
computers and therefore had to adapt at a time when they were already
reasonably well into their working careers. New product and system
designs alongside the need to respond immediately to customer enquiries,
amounted to a series of pressures which required different skills. Staff need
negotiating skills and the ability to consult with people and they are
required to bring a certain amount of flair and confidence to their jobs.

Whilst some customers were thought to be a little suspicious at times
vis-à-vis the counter technology, at the same time they did expect it to
work and for the counter staff to be able to make it work! Staff have to learn
to carry detail in their heads and to be able to interpret statistics. Although
thorough product and technology handling is a continuous and on-going
activity, the reason for the higher turnover rate for the late 30s and over age

group was thought to be the demands of work which required significantly
different skills.

Implications for the personnel function
The observation of the impact of technical change on employees in this
way has meant a change to recruitment policy. The employee specification
has been revised upwards. 'Higher quality staff' are required and one of the
main qualities necessary is 'personality'. There are a number of restric-
tions on the implementation of this policy. Staff stability rates are high at
between 80 and 90 per cent over the last decade. In a small branch of just
three or four people turnover rate may be extremely low. The supply of
new staff with the appropriate combination of four or five 'O' levels and
the required personal qualities has also become extremely small. All the
building societies, banks and other financial institutions are in the same
market for the same potential employees!

The approach to staff shortfalls such as these is to move staff into
different jobs in the same branch or to second them to another branch.
Decision making at this level is the responsibility of the district and branch
managers. Those with the requisite personality and confidence are placed
in prominent counter positions.

Employee Commitment

Well developed consultation structures have been in use at the Woolwich
Equitable Building Society for many years. Central, Regional and Departmental meetings between the staff association and managers are held on
a regular basis.

Mandatory staff meetings are held by all managers on a monthly
basis. In addition personnel policy is to operate an open door strategy and
to undertake periodic 'walkabouts'. If personnel professionals are understood by employees to be visible and accessible, then it is generally found
that any employee or employee relations problem will fairly quickly
become known to them.

Staff Association Reactions

No new technology agreement has been either requested or negotiated
with the staff association. This was thought to be unnecessary because of

already well understood flexibility and mobility requirements, and the existence of good work management practices.

The earlier job mobility clause in the letter of engagement had previously been accepted in principle by the staff association, although it was subject to individual ability and department/branch requirements. However, the enforcement of equal opportunities *vis-à-vis* mobility requirements for all employees has been established in the last few years. In addition, employees' attention is now drawn to flexibility requirements particularly in the letters of appointment for head office appointments.

Staff association representatives accept the place and pace of changing technology in the organization. As organizational growth is a factor running alongside technical change, the 'last resort' position that employees face is more likely to be relocation to another branch or department than job loss. The redundancy policy, agreed more than a decade ago, has never been implemented in spite of a number of organizational changes.

Displaced Staff

As information technology is changing the character of certain jobs, so jobs lost in one area are created in another. New branches and developments are on stream and the Woolwich has a current vacancy rate of between one and two hundred. Displaced staff are redeployed within the organization and it is notable that the staff turnover rate has been between 10 per cent and 12 per cent in the last few years until the merger and current levels are about 15 per cent.

The head office at Woolwich has been operating in some localized areas with manual systems but computerized systems are rapidly replacing them in the short term future. However, the reduction in staff numbers will be achieved by a combination of natural wastage over a period of time and secondly, by transfer to branches which are being increased in number every year, besides the development of new activities.

Many data processing staff have been recruited externally, but others have been transferred from head office administrative staff after skills tests identified those who would be responsive to training for data processing.

Payment Systems

Two job grading committees consider grading claims for new or restructured jobs on an on-going basis. In anticipation of a series of claims for

regrading on the basis of the changes in counter staff's skills and responsibilities, it is accepted that eventually an overall review of regrading will
be conducted. However, how much regrading will actually take place is a
matter for the future. Whilst staff have acquired new responsibilities such
as the interpretation of statistics, other activities such as clerical work have
been largely removed from the workload. The current result is a quid
pro quo.

The 400 data processor staff have their own salary structure, which
is reviewed twice a year.

Annual negotiations normally lead to a market comparison increase
and settlement to be awarded in October of each year. Previously, each
April an incremental award was agreed based on the judgement of line
managers on the performance of staff. Increments were worth between 0
and 6 per cent of salary, with 3 per cent being the most frequent award.

A new appraisal system has now been introduced with the overall
intention of achieving a closer link between performance and pay,
appraisal and annual increments. The previous appraisal system had been
operating for 17 years without review and it was thought to be important
to provide line managers with a real link between the appraisal interview
and pay. It was also intended to influence high flying staff and, at the
opposite pole, those who were in effect being paid for 'being there'!

Performance rating is completed twice, once on the judgement of the
line manager and once on the self assessment of the member of staff. An
overall rating of between one and six is then agreed at interviews, relating
to ten factors such as 'Knowledge and Skills', 'Customers', 'Managing
Systems', 'Prioritizing Work'. An overall total up to a maximum of 60
points is then correlated with a payments scale. Essentially those scoring
under 30 receive no increments, and those scoring between 42 and 49 at the
top of the range, receive the maximum of two increments with those
scoring over 50 a 5 per cent bonus in addition.

The operation of the new appraisal system will mean further final
devolution of decision making to branch level. Branch managers already
have had responsibility for most personnel matters in consultation with the
Regional Personnel Officers. They have previously had responsibility for
the recruitment of staff up to the first supervisory level, although their
management activities generally are closely monitored. The new appraisal
scheme gives branch managers the opportunity to control an appraisal
system which links reward to effort.

Personnel Management

Personnel managers have seen a recent dramatic effect on their workload. Over a period 1,250 vacancies have had to be filled, with between 200 and 300 vacancies current at any one time. Retirement age has been reduced to 60 from 62 to come into line with female retirement age and this means that a larger number of staff have been leaving the society this year. However a major area of activity has been that of training provision for managers and for staff in the areas of new products, new technology and customer service.

The Assistant General Manager (Personnel) in conjunction with the Training and Development Manager has overall responsibility for manpower planning. This is thought of as an 'up-front' operation. Personnel information, systems and training planning form part of a co-ordinated manpower strategy. Full personnel details are available to the Training Manager who acts upon them as soon as possible to ensure all staff are developed to the best of their abilities.

Currently 42 staff are fully engaged in training provision and the Woolwich has its own residential training centre. Branch managers have much responsibility for the co-ordination and implementation of local training. Each branch is closed for half an hour each week so that staff can be trained in a range of requirements including new computer systems and new product ranges. In 1986/87 40 per cent of staff attended customer service based courses at an off the job location for two or three days depending on their status. 34 per cent attended new services training at off-the-job centres. Many courses are regionally based and all are organized by the Training Department.

Employees have shown a continued enthusiasm to be included on training courses. Fifteen years ago very few people wanted to be sent on courses, but in 1987/88 demand is constant! Since the mid 1970s women in particular have become more enthusiastic about off-the-job training generally. Career prospects are open to them up to Executive level but most appointments occur to Manager, Customer Services, level. All jobs are advertised throughout the Society and have been since 1970, thus allowing staff to consider job prospects and their future.

Since the assurance of confidentiality is one of the working rules of personnel procedures, the increased use of computerized systems can place this rule under some strain. Computer auditors, when working on personnel systems are carefully supervised and allowed restricted access only as appropriate.

Personnel officers are brought in if 'industrial relations' problems arise at branch level in connection with new technology. Personnel officers assess in conjunction with line management whether judgments made are either right or wrong but in the final analysis they respect that management has to manage. Many difficulties experienced with new technology or other matters at branch level are often found to be due to a failure of communications of both sides and matters can be eased by explanation.

Conclusion

Over the last few years a wide range of opinions have been publicly expressed on the likely impact of changing technology on employee relations in terms of both personnel management and the individual employee. In 1985–6 the Institute set out to ascertain the likely effect of robotics in the manufacturing sector against a background of warnings that millions of workers would be displaced from their jobs and widespread unemployment ensue. The results of that survey indicated a number of significant and far-reaching changes in the perceived role of personnel management in those organizations which had taken steps towards introducing computer-controlled manufacturing processes (see the Introduction). This book goes a stage further and looks at comparative evidence in a cross-section of 24 dynamic organizations (of which 16 are represented in the case studies) covering not only the manufacturing sector but services and finance, retail and distribution, and the public sector including utilities.

The picture that emerges is one of accelerating change. Where a few years ago the effects of changing technology were being felt in particular sectors of industry, it was now widespread both in its extent and speed of introduction. A glance at the headlines of the employment section of any national paper reveals the revolution taking place. The following appeared in the *Financial Times* in the four weeks before going to press (May 1989):

- 'ICI to alter managerial training and pay format' (proposals aimed at creating a new work culture designed to encourage flexibility and skill development)
- 'Retail and service staff face revised working patterns' (including annualized hours, 'nil' hours and temporary work contracts)
- 'Manual workers "being chosen by new methods"' (which test flexibility, willingness to work in teams, and the ability to be re-trained for new tasks)

- 'Shifts in clerical staff status forecast' (increasing use and sophistication of computer technology will produce big changes in their type of work and status)

- 'Workforce buys bus group in share deal' (one of the first sales of a company involving an employee share ownership plan since the new Budget made such schemes more attractive).

The effect of change in the various sectors of employment is so diverse that it makes generalizations dangerous. In addition, it is unrealistic to isolate technological change from changes induced by the economy, the market or deliberate management policy. One sector may have to face a long period of slimming down its workforce and another sudden and large-scale redundancies, while others are building up a new workforce on a greenfield site. Some interesting comparative figures are quoted in a recent report on the Scottish electronics industry:[1]

> Between 1979 and 1987 the banking, finance and insurance sector of the Scottish economy created an additional 42 thousand jobs: equal to the entire existing employment of the electronics industry. Over the same period production industries in Scotland excluding electronics lost 236 thousand jobs: equal to about 180 jobs for every new job created in electronics over the period.

All one can say with any certainty is that, in the absence of the introduction of new technology, employment figures would probably have been *lower* because the plants would have been at an even greater competitive disadvantage.

Change, with the diversification it brings, is driven by investment; and investment is on such a huge scale (installing sophisticated computer-controlled plant often runs into hundreds of millions of pounds) that there is a new focus on long-term planning and overall strategy. This in turn has an effect on management style, which (as noted in the comment on some of the case studies) tends to move from the traditional chain of command to a more integrated group approach to achieving common strategic objectives. The personnel management functions change along with those of line management.

Other clear trends noted in almost every case study are the need for job flexibility, training and communication. Each of these puts the emphasis on the individual rather than the collective. In place of skilled and semi-skilled workers with a common apprenticeship in their particular craft, there is a growing need for multi-skilled individuals trained to operate sophisticated plant in a way which may be unique to that particular organization; hence the prime importance of training and face-to-face communication. All this points to less use of pay comparisons, a decline in the concept of parity and a new emphasis on performance-related pay. Yet the group psychology cannot be ignored. There are deep-rooted feelings of 'fairness' which increasingly require the personnel manager to ensure co-ordination between departments and sites within the organization.

Where in all this is a role for trade unions and the part of the personnel function that deals with them? It is tempting to look for a 'blueprint' in the case studies on how the employee relations of change should be handled; but there is none. There is a remarkable diversity of practice among the most successful organizations, including those in the case studies. Some do not recognize any union, others recognize only one in a 'single union' agreement, and a number not only recognize several unions but accept a situation of 100% membership on a voluntary basis. With the emphasis on change to maintain international competitiveness and the viability of the organization, it is the strategic objectives which form the common element, not the methods of getting there – which are as variable as the history and circumstances of each separate organization.

One of the most commonly quoted strategic objectives is 'quality'. Yet in pursuit of product or service quality it is clear that the over-riding ingredient for success is not the organizational structure, the payment systems, the group and individual employee relations policies, but the *quality of management* acting as an integrated team. The personnel manager, as a member of that team, is one of the prime agents of effective change: a planner of human resources, co-ordinator of line management personnel functions, and integrator of personnel policies which are in tune with the overall strategic objectives.

Reference

1   John MacInnes and Alan Sproull, 'Union recognition and employment change in Scottish electronics', *Industrial Relations Journal*, Vol. 20, No. 1 (Spring 1989).